JESUS' GUIDE TO DIVINE HEALING

A Step by Step Guide to Healing

By: Ferd Sebastian, as he
was taught by the Holy Spirit.

ISBN: 1456327437
ISBN-13: 9781456327439

Dedication & Appreciation

To my wife Beverly, who is a part of me.

Gen 2:24
Therefore shall a man leave his father and his mother, and shall cleave unto his wife: and they shall be one flesh.

Beverly, put up with me through my transition as I was being Born Again, into a Man of God. It took love and patience and great faith which she has, for sometimes I knew that she must have thought that I was going crazy.

To Men of God

Smith Wigglesworth, John Lake, Brother Kenneth Hagin, F.F. Bosworth. These men all blazed a trail to Faith and Healing.

To my Teacher, Savior and Constant Companion, Jesus And His Holy Spirit.

John 14:26
But the Comforter, which is the Holy Spirit, whom the Father will send in my name, he shall teach you all things, and bring all things to your remembrance, whatsoever I have said unto you.

 He would wake me up at 5:00 in the morning and say you need to put in this or that and then would stay with me until I got it right... At times I wrote things that I had no way of knowing. I just said, "Thank you Jesus", for guiding me. Praise God".

The things that I began to do I questioned. Was I exceeding my authority? I did not want to be presumptuous. Jesus was the one who was doing the work. Not me. Still I was hesitant for a long time until Jesus showed me who I was in Him.

John 15:16 You have not chosen me, but I have chosen you, and ordained you, that you should go and bring forth fruit, and that your fruit should remain: that whatsoever you shall ask of the Father in my name, he may give it to you.

There are not enough words to properly show my appreciation to Jesus for what He has given me. Thank you, Jesus.

To My Readers

You are starting on an adventure into the Spiritual World. We will be opening a door to Heaven. Your Guide will be Jesus!

If you are a Child in Christ, you will grow in Wisdom

If you are a Mature Christian, you will re-establish your Faith.

If you have never known Jesus before, you are Beginning a Wonderful Journey into Health and Happiness!

God Bless You and may you receive,
Wisdom and Knowledge in His Word!

I want you to get four things out of these lessons.

1) How to get Divine Healing for yourself.
2) How to minister Divine Healing to the sick.
3) How to walk in Divine Health.
4) The most important: How to have a close relationship with Jesus.

The Following is how I found Jesus and His purpose for my life.

Table of Content

Chapter 1

Praise Reports

Terminal Cancer

Hi Ferd,

Nobody can mistake the Power of Our Lord God! Over a year ago I was told that I had cancer and would need treatment for it. Then about six months ago I was told it was Terminal... Incurable... And that the Holidays coming up would be my last.

Then through a friend of mine, Ferd was told about my problem and called me, out of a clear blue sky. We talked for the longest time and yet I had never met the man or ever talked or heard about him before that miracle night.

Ferd, asked me if he could pray for my healing, and after talking with him for a while I knew that was what I wanted also. After we prayed, Ferd said, if I truly believed then God has healed me.

I am here to tell you I truly believe in the Power of Our Lord God... And yes, I am healed.

I went to the Doctors and they informed me I had no sign of Cancer in any of the tests they performed.

We must never give up, or stop believing, in the Power of our God and His Son, Jesus Christ.

Sincerely,
Ray Dresser

Diseased Heart

This is a note from Roma Jones, a 60 year old woman that had a diseased heart. So bad, heart transplant looked like the only answer. But Roma, like the woman with the issue of blood, came searching for Jesus the Healer and found Him.............

Dear Brother Ferd,

What a report!!! Just Praising God for the HEALING!! Just look at my report! Wait until I give my testimony! We are doing great. See you sometime this summer.

Roma and Richard

<u>Here is Roma's report!</u>

PREVENTION PLUS, INC.
STROKE & ARTERIAL SCRERENING

Study Location: Villages
Dateof Study: 5/12/04

Dear Mrs. Jones,

Thank you for your participation at our recent screening. Enclosed you will find written reports of your various screening. If you have any questions please don't hesitate to call our office for assistance.

Normal No Abnormalites

On the basis of this screening, you echocardigram results are as follows....
Normal on the basis of this screening all measuurements and observations appear normal with no abnormalities. Negative stenisosis, negitive regurritation, negitive mitral valxe prolapse, negitive leaflet calcifications, negitive pericordial effusion (fluid around heart), negitive enlargements, left venntricular wall appears normal.

HIV Positive, Needed Jesus

Jeanne, a single young lady came to me on 2jesus, HIV positive and this is the prayer we prayed together.

Dear Father, Jeanne, is sorry and asks your forgiveness. Jeanne, is also not going to have promiscuous sex again. Jeanne and I come to you for healing of HIV. Father we are asking that you heal Jeanne completely. That Jeanne's body will be new again. That all of the HIV will be cast out, we command it to shrivel up and die and be cast out of Jeanne's body... We command this in the name of Jesus. We pray that Jeanne's body will be filled with your love and power. Let the Holy Spirit burn brightly in Jeanne so that the world will not just see Jeanne anymore but will just see your love shining out of her. We know that Jesus died on the cross for our sins, and He also took our diseases to the cross. (Matt. 817) He took our infirmities and carried our diseases! Jesus said, (Mark 11:23-24) that if we have faith and do not doubt, that it will be done. Therefore when we ask, believe that we have received it. Father we know that you heard us and we know that Jeanne is now healed. So Father we thank you and forever praise your holy name. We pray this prayer in Jesus name to the Father so that His Son Jesus will be glorified and bring glory to the Father, Your loving children, Jeanne and Ferd. Amen!

Jeanne, you are healed, your HIV will start leaving your body, it may be gone now or it might take a few weeks. The time it takes to get out is

related to how strong your faith is. Now you made a promise to God about the promiscuous sex. Keep it... I mean KEEP IT!!!   Least a worse thing come upon you...John 5:14
In Christ, Ferd

Jeanne's Testimony 2 weeks later.

Hi Ferd,

I want to thank you so much for your prayer a couple of weeks ago. I received blood test results from my doctor and I tested negative for HIV. That is completely ruled out... PRAISE GOD! He really does hear our prayers and I'm so grateful to Him. My body was displaying all symptoms of the virus and even doctors were saying that it was HIV, but God had the last word, and I knew that. I thank God for His mercy and His grace and the preservation of my life and future. I also thank Him for sustaining me through the toughest time in my life to date. He helped me out of a mess I mistakenly created for myself and put me back on solid ground. I'll never stray from Him again and I make a conscious effort to always put Him first in my life. Thank you God for all you've done for me, my family, and friends. I can now call this a lesson learned and look forward to a bright future.

Thank you again Ferd.
Jeanne

Kathy Ann, Leukemia testimony

Two girls in Gadsden Prison where my wife and I have a Christian ministry, Saving Racing Greyhounds and Healing Broken Spirits, wanted a Divine Healing book, one like you are about to read. So I asked the program director if they could have one and she said yes. So next trip I took them up. Then a month later we went up again. Here is what we found.

While we were gone another girl that I had not met before was put into our group. She had leukemia. Well one of my girls gave her the Divine Healing book and said that she should read it. Her name was Kathy Ann.   When I came in Kathy Ann was there to greet me. She was like a bright light, all aglow.

Kathy said that she opened my book and read about the man with terminal cancer, that was the first testimony in this chapter and how Jesus healed him. She said, "I took the book and for the next two days I did noting but read it over and over and was just absorbing God's word."

The week before we came she went to her regular doctor's appointment. Praise God there was no trace of Leukemia. I laid my hand on her head and we both praised God and thanked Jesus for the healing.

Michelle.... also a Prison Inmate, came into prison HIV Positive

Michelle was one of the two girls that had originally asked for the healing book. She did not tell me at the time that she was HIV Positive. She told me later that she wanted one just because I had given one to Dixie, another Inmate who is a strong believer.

So Michelle said she browsed through it and put it aside. Then when Kathy Ann came in and was worried about her Leukemia, Michelle gave it to her to read. Well when Kathy Ann got healed it really woke Michelle up. She took the book back and started to really read it.

So many people do not think Divine Healing is really possible, until they see someone who has gotten healed. Then they say, "what about me." So Michelle then read the book in a new light... BELIVIVG!

I do not have to tell you. You know... Michelle is no longer HIV Positive and when we see her now in prison, she is praising God and shouting for joy. Her real fear was that she would die in prison and she would never have a life again. Jesus has changed that, Thank you Jesus.

My name is Ferd Sebastian. I get letters and testimonies like this all the time. And I am here to tell you that the Glory belongs to Him. **Jesus Christ, is The Healer**. Jesus has let me be His voice, to say His words, and to help, His children. For this I praise God.

Rev. 12:11 We overcome the Devil by the Blood of the Lamb and the word of our testimony. I will use testimonies throughout this book that I have been connected with. Not to show how great I am. For without Jesus I am nothing. But to give you faith that Jesus is alive and well. That He is with us HEALING today as He was 2000 years ago.

Hebrew 13:8 Jesus Christ is the same yesterday and today and forever. Jesus has been with me all of my life, but I only started walking with Him in 1989. The following is my walk with Jesus; many times He had to carry me. Thank you Jesus!

Prov 4:20-22

20 My son, attend to my words; incline thine ear unto my sayings.

21 Let them not depart from thine eyes; keep them in the midst of thine heart.

22 For they are life unto those that find them, and health to all their flesh.

<u>We get healed by following God's word!</u>

The following information is all from the Bible. Jesus picked me up from the door of death. Healed me, and then called me to help others. He blessed me everyday with His Wisdom and Patience. He led me by the hand, step at a time,
as He still does.....Thank you Jesus!

Chapter 2

This Is Why I Know God's Word Is True Ferd's Testimony

At this time I am now 77 years old, however I feel like I am in my prime. I had wasted most of my life fighting the world, trying to get ahead. Twenty two years ago, in 1988, I found I was not Superman. There was always someone faster, meaner, or uglier to aggravate my life. After pounding my body to the breaking point I was brought to my knees. My heart was clogged up from stress and improper eating. I needed open heart surgery! But I wasn't whipped yet. I had money. So I told my Doctor to get the best surgeon, which he did and my operation was a success.

However after six months, my bypasses stopped up again. I got the bad news. I was down for the count. The doctors said my best chance would be if they blocked off or killed half of my heart. I would be severally restricted in my activity, (they meant I could do nothing) I could die in the operation, but that if I didn't do it I was sure to have a massive heart attack which would kill me. I told them I would let them know my decision and left.

I was a film producer living in Los Angeles at that time, so dejectedly I went to the studio. However Jesus jolted me. A thought came as clear as day. Ferd, you can't handle this. There is nothing you or your money can do. You need help. Then a voice said, **"Jesus is the answer."** I asked my son and wife if they would pray with me and we went out to a vacant sound stage. As we were walking out to the stage, I remembered something my father told me as a child. That Jesus made promises to his followers. One of them was answering prayers. I was 55 years old at the time of my heart problems, and I hadn't been to church or picked up a Bible in probably 40 years. But I wanted to claim Jesus' promise. So we prayed to Jesus to heal me. I said the world's simplest prayer. "Jesus please heal me." I felt a small snap in my chest. Jesus reached down and picked me up and said. **"Why didn't you call on me sooner? I've been with you all the time, but you wouldn't listen."** So He healed my body, renewed my mind, and filled me with praise...

From that day on I got stronger. I told the doctors, Jesus had healed me. They didn't believe me. They gave me a test where they put a radio active solution in my veins and photographed my heart. It was healed. I had full circulation. They told me that something else must have happened, but I knew Jesus was a man of his word, even if I didn't know where the word was. That was the start of waking me up to Jesus. I had not been putting Jesus first in my life. Jesus was lucky to be in fifth place after work, money, family and play. In other words, I though of Him very seldom. But he had not forgotten me. He gave me the chance to live and I thank Him with every breath.

For two years after my healing, I had been thanking God... But that was all. Then in 1990 in my home I had a vision... I met Jesus and He filled me with His Spirit. After this I was so filled with compassion, I had to share what I had... My testimony... **Rev. 12:11, They defeated him (the Devil) by the Blood of Jesus and their testimony.**

I wanted to help other people so I started to testify to heart patients as my main ministry as I could relate to how they felt, and I wanted them to know what happened to me. At that time I didn't know why my prayer worked. I started reading the Bible and asking God to make His word clear to me. It became interesting to me and I started reading it like a novel. It never made much sense to me before but now it did. From a Minister in California, I learned that the Bible was God talking to me. I also found that every time I read the Bible I learned something new. I will read a particular book, say John that I have read many times before and find something that I wonder how that got there. How could I have missed that? The only thing I can think of is God kept opening my mind and revealing new things to me. Thank God for His teaching, now I can better serve other people by going over with them passages in the Bible.

I wanted more than anything to show other people how to be healed. I studied how Jesus healed. I ask the Holy Spirit to teach me and He did. Then I ask Jesus to send me someone that He thought I could help. He sent a man who just walked up to me and said, "I do not know why I am here." I said, "tell me is something wrong." He said, "I am going to die tomorrow and I am scared." I said, "I know why you are here come, sit down." (If you work for Jesus, ask for His help.)

---------------Paul-------------

In the past the man had the same operation that they wanted to give me. They had killed half of his heart. Now the other half was dying and they were going to operate in the morning. They gave him no hope. Like me he had been away from Jesus all of his adult life. It was like looking in a mirror at myself. I shared Jesus with him, and showed him the things that I am going to teach you. Then we prayed. He left happy, even if he died he knew he was saved. The next morning at 8 AM he was in the hospital prepped and ready to go in for the operation when a doctor came in and examined him. He left and at 9AM he came back with two other doctors and they examined him. At 11AM his surgeon came in and he examined him. The surgeon told him to put his clothes on and go home, to come back in six months for a check up. There was nothing the matter with his heart. Even the dead half was working perfectly. **Praise God.** I do not know which I liked best, my healing or being part of God's work and seeing that man healed. This was the start of telling many people about Jesus' Divine Healing. And many have been healed.

In 1996, my Doctor told me my lab reports indicated that I had prostate cancer. What did I want to do about it? I told him I would be back in a month and take another test. I went home and prayed to Jesus to heal me. After 30 days I went back to the Doctor to take another test. The test was NEGATIVE. **Praise The Lord!** I now added Cancer patients to my list and many have been healed.

------------Laura & Mike------------
Daryl, a friend of mine had heard about the heart healing of Laura Mohammed, the mother of a boy that worked with him. She was going in for a heart transplant, but never had to go... We shared Jesus and she got a new heart, from the Divine Physician..... Daryl, ask if I would pray with a young man, Mike, with terminal brain cancer. Daryl and I met at his apartment and we shared Jesus' teachings with him. Then I went to Alaska on a trip. While there the Lord told me that Mike was cured. I could not wait to get back and tell him. When I got back I called to tell him. But he already knew. The Doctor had given him another MRI to see how fast it was growing. The terminal cancer was gone. Vanished! **Thank Jesus.**

When I was 64 years old, I had a stroke. My left side was paralyzed with no feeling. You could drive a nail thorough my arm and leg and I would not feel it. My wife called 911 for an ambulance to take me to the hospital. While we were waiting we all prayed together for Jesus to heal me. Before we were through with the prayer my left arm and leg started tingling. I didn't even get to say Amen. By the time the ambulance arrived I could walk and I had all my feelings back.

PRAISE GOD, I LOVE JESUS SO MUCH. HE HAS BEEN SO GOOD TO ME!

They took me to the hospital and gave me a cat scan; they were looking for the clot. I told them they would not find it. Jesus took it away. They didn't find it, but this time, I think one of the nurses believed me. They kept me in the hospital three days for observation, everything was OK. My wife picked me up to go home and on the way we decided to stop for lunch. The owner of the small cafe was a friend of mine and was concerned about my being in the hospital. I told him not to worry Jesus healed me. He asked would I talk to his cook. His father had just had a stroke and the boy was terribly worried about him. I turned to my wife and said, "Now I know that having my stroke like my other two illnesses was a blessing."

Now I've got a whole new group to minister too. If you are a Christian, God can always turn your misfortunes into blessings. Use your misfortune. Pay attention and use these lessons in life to build faith and to glorify God.

James 1:2-4 Consider it pure joy, my brothers, whenever you face trials of many kinds, because you know that the testing of your faith develops perseverance. Perseverance must finish its work so that you may be mature and complete, not lacking anything

Tongues, 1997: As I progressed with Jesus I read in Acts about tongues. I also searched out Churches that believed in healing. They almost always believed in tongues. I had been told as a child to stay away from people like that. They could be of the Devil.

I was reading Acts in bed one night and thought... If it is in the Bible... It is true. The Bible is either true or it is not! So I ask Jesus. "Is this for me?" "If so I want it." Immediately I started speaking in tongues. I was afraid to stop. I might not be able to start again. Then I stopped and started again. I did this again and again. Thank God this was for me.

Jesus himself had filled me with His Spirit years before... But my mind had been set against tongues and I needed the knowledge before I could believe. You cannot believe beyond your knowledge. You must have Spiritual knowledge to have faith in God's promises. **Hosea 4:6 My children are destroyed for lack of knowledge.**

My ministry became jet propelled. I had unbound my spirit. The Holy Spirit was praying with me and was clearing a path before me with my prayers. I started 2jesus.org and the miracles flowed, bringing Jesus the glory. Thank you Father!

You have the POWER to help other people!

(John 14:12-14,) Jesus says, "I tell you the truth, anyone who has faith in me will do what I have

been doing. He will do even greater things than these, because I am going to the Father. And I will do whatever you ask in my name, <u>so that the Son will bring glory to the Father.</u> You may ask anything in My name, and I will do it."

<u>Not you... But the Son will bring glory to the Father.</u> So if you let Jesus, He will use you. (Work through you...) I'm not trying to claim that anything I do is Christ like however; I do have FAITH and TRUST in JESUS.

Thank God that when He looks at me, He does not see this faulty person I am. All He sees is the Christ that lives inside of me and to God that makes me perfect.

Why did I get all of these ailments? God certainly didn't give them to me. No, that would be counter productive, and that isn't how God operates. God doesn't make you sick, just so He could heal you. No we live in the Devils world and he is here to kill you. By the time you are 77, you will probably have one or more of these illnesses also. Will you let them kill you? Or do you want to live? Don't wait as long as I did to find the key to health and happiness in this lifetime.

"Ferd" I got all of these illnesses over a 10 year period. Through Jesus I had learned how to heal myself, but not how to stay well. Now I daily claim God's promises and I stay well... The devil will try to put something on me but praise God now I have the knowledge of God and can cast the disease out of my life.

Psalm 91: 1) He who dwells in the shelter of the Most High will rest in the shadow of the Almighty. 2) I will say of the Lord, "He is my refuge and my fortress, my God in whom I trust."

Read the rest of this psalm, it is a wonderful promise for us from God...

My Second Vision

I was just leaving a restaurant where my wife and I ate, she saw a man holding onto a column and said, "Ferd you should help him." I spoke with him, he said he had MS and was having a seizure. He could not stand without the column. I laid hands on him and prayed and he got his strength back, thanked me and went to his car. I followed him out to make sure he was alright. His wife who was in the car came out and helped him into the car then she thanked me.

As I watched them leave I spoke to Jesus, I said, "Why me? You are always there to help me." I had certainly had not lived a perfect life.... Then Jesus showed me why... This was my second vision, right there in the parking lot. My life started flashing before me just like a movie. I was a baby and my parents were praying for me. I was a young man and they were praying for me. I was in the Military and they were praying for me. I was making movies in Hollywood and they were praying for me. Then I saw my father's funeral and then he was standing beside Jesus and my father was talking to Jesus about me. It was as clear as day. I instantly knew everything... My parents had prayed for me every day of my life. Even after death I saw that they were with Jesus... Taking me before Him, so pray for your children... Jesus listens.

Chapter 3

The Way to Receive Jesus' Divine Healing Power

God can heal anyone He wants too, any time He wants too, as He is moved. Like Jesus, at the pool of Bethesda, John 5:2. Jesus had compassion and came to the crippled man. Just think. He had to step over many who were ill, to get to the one He wanted. It is wonderful if God picks you to be healed. But we cannot depend on that for our healing. If you are sick you want to be healed. And you want to be sure you will get it... We do not want to wait for God to get to us. We want to know that we can go to God. And every time we go to God, we will get our healing. How do we do that?

We go by God's Word. And come in faith, Jesus has given us specific promises that are ours. If we know the promises and meet His conditions, He will heal us. No ifs and no maybes. Otherwise He may or may not depending on how He is moved. So to be sure we must follow God's rules and promises. God, will do what He says. A Promise is a Promise and He can not lie. Hebrews 6:18

The Devil wants to keep you from God's word. He will try to confuse you and put doubts into your head. He will try to use human logic.

Colossians 2:8-9, See to it that no one takes you captive through hollow and deceptive philosophy, which depends on human tradition

and the basic principals of this world rather than Christ. 9) For in Christ all the fullness of the Deity lives in bodily form, and you have been given fullness in Christ, who is the head over every power and authority.

2 Cor. 5:7 For we walk by faith, not by sight. (Or human logic.)

Here is the way to be sure you receive Jesus' Divine Healing

1. Believe in Jesus Christ.   John 3:16 For God so loved the world, that He gave His only begotten Son, that whosoever believed in Him should not perish, but have everlasting life.

2. Believe in the Bible. The Bible is God Talking to you. **Acts 20:32 And now brethren, I commend you to God, and to the Word of His grace, which is able to build you up, and to give you an** inheritance **among all them which are sanctified.** Inheritance. **YOU ARE A SON OR DAUGHTER OF GOD AND ALL OF HIS GIFTS ARE YOURS!** But a gift is no good if you do not know you have it. You must find your gifts and accept them. That is what we will be doing.

3. Psalms. 37:5 Delight yourself also in the Lord; and He shall give you the desires of your heart. Commit your way unto the Lord; trust also in Him; and He shall bring it to pass. Delight yourself in the Lord... How do we do that? By reading His words and loving Him, and making Him part of our life, **and acting on His Word.**

My son, attend to my words; incline your ears unto my sayings. Let them not depart from your eyes; keep them in the midst of your heart (in your spirit). For they are life unto those that find them, and health to all their flesh. Prov. 4:20-22

4. Be certain no doubt is in your life. The devil wants to tell you this is not true. He wants you weak and sick and filled with doubts. It is natural to have doubtful thoughts just don't give in to them. **(I pray daily for God to keep the devil out of my life and to have his angels watch over me.) (I say Jesus is my salvation, Jesus is my healer and Jesus is the light of my life. My reason for being, the love of my life! I say my body, soul, and spirit belongs to Jesus! The Devil has no place or control in or over my life.)**

Romans 10:10 For it is with your heart that you believe and are justified, and it is with your mouth that you confess and are saved..........
    When you confess what you are in Christ, claim it, and walk in it, you are appropriating the reality of what is legally yours.
    Proverbs 18:21, The power of life and death are in the tongue.
    Constantly confess that God's word is true. GOD'S WORDS ARE TRUE!
    James 1:6-7. But let him ask in faith, nothing wavering. For he that wavers is like a wave of the

sea driven with the wind and tossed. For let not that man think that he shall receive anything of the Lord.

Jesus tells us in Mark 11:23 "I tell you the truth, if anyone says to this mountain, go through yourself into the sea, and does not doubt in his heart but believes that what he says will happen, it will be done for him."

That is very strong... What Jesus is saying is that the Holy Spirit is going to perform what you ask, if you have faith and if it lines up with the word of God.

Jesus is speaking to Christians here, His disciples. He knows that we as Christians would not knowingly ask for something that God would not want us to have. So does God want you healed? We will get to that in just a little bit. What I want you to learn here is to make your confessions positive and to line up with God's word.

To confess something negative would put the Devil back in control. And we want him out of your life. He is the reason for your illness.

5. Ask God to forgive your sins. Before you ask God for something, "get right with Him." If you have any hate in your heart, get rid of it. Forgive anyone you might be mad at. Confess your sins to God and pray in Jesus name and you will be forgiven.

Matthew 6:14 For if you forgive men their trespasses, your heavenly Father will also forgive you. ..1 John 1:9 If we confess our sins He is faithful

and just and will forgive us our sins and purify us from all unrighteousness.

Mark 2:9 Jesus said, "Which is easier to say, your sins are forgiven or get up and take your mat and walk?" Jesus is telling us that when you are healed you are forgiven. So if we know this, would it not be nice to show we want to do what is right and ask forgiveness before we ask for healing.

Sin, can will bring on sickness, because you are letting the Devil take control. It is up to us to cast the Devil out of our lives. Jesus gave us this power. Mark 16:17

6. Now does God promise what you are asking for? Faith begins where the will of God is known. Faith must rest on the will of God alone, not on our desires or wishes. **Appropriating faith is not believing God can, but that He will!** Find the scripture where Jesus has promised your healing and use it in your prayer.

Such as: Matthew 8:17 Himself took our infirmities, and bare our sickness.

1 Peter 2:24 Who his own self bare our sins in his own body on the tree, that we being dead to sins, should live unto righteousness: by whose stripes we are healed. Prov. 4:20 My words are life unto those that find them and health to all their flesh. Psalm 107:20 He sent His Word and healed them. (Jesus is the word.. John 1:1 In the beginning was the Word and the Word was with God.) **Psalm 103:3 Who forgives all your sins and heals all your disease. Psalm 50:15 "call upon Me**

in the day of trouble: I will deliver thee and thou shall glorify Me." Jesus as well as bearing our sins, took all of our sickness with him to the cross. What a wonderful thing as Christians to know we do not have to be sick. All we have to do is claim what God has promised us. And what a terrible thing for Jesus to have to bear all of our diseases and we don't even take advantage of the sacrifice He made for us. If you are unsure of this, ask yourself, is it God's will to keep His promises?

7. What did Christ really do for us, concerning healing, when he went to the cross?

Galatians 3:13, "Christ hath redeemed us from the curse of the law, being made a curse for us: Colossians 1:13 For He has rescued us from the Dominion of Darkness and brought us into the Kingdom of the Son He loves. (Jesus rescued us but if we do not know this, the Devil will eat you alive!)

There is no sickness in the Kingdom of the Son!

What was the curse of the law? **God's laws was threefold: Poverty, Sickness, Death. Spiritual death.** Satan lost dominion over our lives the minute we were born again. **Romans 6:14, "For sin shall not have dominion over you: for you are not under the law, but under grace."** Therefore, because we are no longer dominated by Satan... Now disease can no longer lord it over us. **We need to believe that. Then we can start talking about it! Then it** will become a reality in our spirits. **Revelation 12:11, says, "And they overcame him (Satan) by the Blood of the Lamb, and by the word of their testimony."**

If we are born again in Christ, the word is already true in our lives. All we have to do is claim these promises. If you don't know about the spiritual things that are yours, they will not do you any good. **It is what we confess with our lips that really dominate our inner being.**

CONFESS THIS ALOUD: Duet. 28:22, My disease is a curse of the law! BUT! Gal. 3:13 Jesus redeemed us from the curse of the law. Therefore I can command my illness to leave! Say this over and over until it gets out of your mind and into your spirit. Jesus gave us complete control over the Devil and the power to use His name. **Mark 16:17 "in My name they shall drive out demons."** Use it!

8. You can always depend on God's word. If we just have faith. Sounds easy, I didn't know what faith was. I bet you don't either. You probably think it means to believe, wrong. You can believe in something and not have faith in it... You can believe in every word in the Bible, but if you do not act on the word it does you no good. Acting on the Word is faith. **Hebrews ll:1 Now faith is the substance of things hope for, the evidence of things not seen. Faith is knowing what God says is true even though you can't see it. You know it, because Heb. 6:18, says, It is impossible for God to lie.........**

2 Corinthians 5:7, For we walk by faith, not by sight. We have to stop walking by what we see around us and **start walking by God's word. (That is acting on faith.)** We have to have faith in it even if we can't see it. Because God says, it is there, we have it. That's what faith is, trusting God's word over what we see around us. You can be sick and your Doctor can say you will be well soon. You're still sick, but you believe him. Why can't you believe God?

Bible Faith... Sees the Invisible... Believes the Incredible.
And Receives the Impossible.

9. After we pray for healing, do we keep praying day after day? If you truly have faith that God healed you, you are now cured. You do not have to pray this prayer again. God heard you. **1 John 5:14-15 if we ask God for anything according to His will we know He hears us and if He hears us we know we have what we ask of Him. Mark 11:24, says, "When you pray, believe that you receive..... and you shall have..."** To pray it again would mean you didn't believe God gave you what you asked for... If that is what you believe you will not be healed. You may still have the symptoms but you are healed.

Hebrews 11:1. Now faith is the substance of things hope for, the evidence of things not seen. First comes faith, we have to believe God healed us, if we do then the substance or healing will follow.

Your senses will make you doubt. But don't confess these doubts. You are healed. The Dr. may say you have a cancer. You say yes, I may have the symptoms but I am now healed. The word of God says I'm healed and I'm standing on the word! God is removing it. The best way to prove this is to read **Luke 17: 11-19. Jesus told the lepers to go and show themselves to the priest.** They could have said, "Are you crazy, that's a long walk and look at me, I've got leprosy all over me." But they didn't, they did what they were told. They had faith in Jesus, and started walking toward the priest, **(they walked by faith not by sight)** and as they walked, they were healed. One came back to say thanks. **Jesus said, "Your faith has made you whole."** First we have to have faith and trust Gods word. Then God brings the evidence of things hope for into our life. **Simply if we do not trust his word, He is not going to answer our prayers.**

Faith is acting on what we believe!

<u>Take a special notice of this:</u> <u>This is where most Christians get in trouble in their healing. They want to be healed physically first and then thank God. That doesn't take faith. Any atheist could do that. If you are waiting for God to heal you forget it. As far as He is concerned He has already given you your healing. Jesus paid the price for you, 1 Peter 2:24. The ball is now in your court...You have to accept what He gave you. If you have accepted your healing, you will not have to ask for it again.</u> **You just need to start praising and thanking God and walking in His word.** The Lord inhabits the praises

of His children. When Paul and Silas were in prison, Acts 16:25, they started singing and praising. Then the Lord shook the foundation of the prison and opened all the doors. God is working while we're praising. That is when your healing will come. **Your healing will move from the Spirit world into the natural world while you Praise God and walk in His word!**

If you get instant healing thank God. Some people get instant healing and some get gradual healing. So if it doesn't come right now do not think that you are not healed. Keep your faith and belief turned on. So many people are healed and because it does not happen in the first few minutes say, well it didn't work. And that just ended their healing. So trust God! His words are true. If He says you are cured, you are cured. If it is a day, a week or a month in coming trust Him and keep praising.... It is on the way. Keep confessing, you are cured. **Thank you Jesus!**

Your illness is like a wilted flower. You see a plant that is wilted, you water it, and nothing changes. You look at it an hour later still nothing happens. You look at it in the morning and it is strong and beautiful.

That is how God's healing works.

Have faith and thank God for the Living Water!!!! (Jesus)

Faith is the currency of God. We have to keep building it up so when we really need it for cancer, heart trouble, etc. we have it. We build faith by hearing God's word. **Faith comes by hearing and hearing by the word of God. Romans 10:17** And also by living the word of God. **(Acting on it.) After we walk in the word we start trusting it**. We know that when we step off into the unknown He will be there to light the way for us.

After I was first healed, I never prayed for little things. I thought like a savings account, I could use it up. So I would save it for big things. Now I pray for everything. Getting my little prayers answered builds my faith. We live from Glory to Glory!

10. God is going to answer your prayers because you believe and have faith in him. Jesus promised it to you. **Jesus said: If you have the faith of a mustard seed you can move a mountain.** This cancer, heart disease, or stroke is your mountain! MOVE IT! God does not lie! You are God's temple. **Cor. 3:16. Don't you know that you are God's temple and that God's Spirit lives in you? If anyone destroys God's temple, God will destroy him;** (God will destroy the Devil for harming you.) God's temple is sacred, and you are that temple. And God wants his temple to be strong.

11. Now let's look at a prayer. If a person does not line up with the above requirements, pray anyway. Try to get them in line, but it is not for you to judge. God knows how these people will react to healing, you do not. I have had people who were not in line, but were healed. As soon as they were healed, they came into line with God's word. Jesus also healed their soul... Thank you Jesus. Mark 16:18 Jesus said, "They will lay hands on the sick and they will be healed. The sick will be healed. Not just the saved or the pure.

THIS LETTER IS FROM THE DAUGHTER OF A 55 YR OLD WOMAN, GIVEN 4 MO. TO LIVE. CANCER IN ALL MAJOR ORGANS, SHE CAME 2JESUS.ORG FOR HEALING. SHE WAS FILLED WITH HATE AND BITTERNESS. IF I WAS TO JUDGE, I WOULD SAY THIS WOMAN WAS NOT IN LINE WITH GOD'S WORD. BUT I PRAYED IN FAITH AND HERE IS WHAT HAPPENED.

Hi Ferd! My mom's doctor called her case a miracle!!!!!!!!!!!!!!!!!!!!!!!!!!

She wants to know where in Florida you are and so does the Doctor they want to come down there to where you are and give a testimony.

Thank you Ferd.

The Doctor doesn't quite understand how this could happen with my mother, but I am letting him know, and my mom is letting him know. It's God!! My mother was literally raised up from death. As you know the cancer was all over her body. But the Doctor found none. It was gone.

My mom is really on fire for the Lord now, and BELIEVES on Him.

She could barely talk when she came to after the operation and I had asked her if she had heard the good report, and she just pointed to the sky and said "It's God"... I know you are just a man, but she really believes that you had a big part in this. She is a different woman. Actually the other day she called my dad to thank him for doing something or other. She would have never have done that before, I don't hear any malice from her about him or bitterness. That is a miracle in itself.

With all of our love forever
Suzann and Mom

YOU SEE WHEN GOD HEALS. HE ALSO HEALS THE SOUL. MATT. 9:1-5

12. How do we pray?

John 14:6, Jesus said, "I am the way, the truth, and the life. No one comes to the Father except through me."
   John 16:23-24, "Whatsoever you ask the Father in my name He will give to you. Ask and you shall receive, that your joy may be full."
   So we pray in the name of Jesus... Plus we always put God's word in remembrance.... We want to remind God of the promises we are standing on. (Show God you took the time to read His word.)
   Isaiah 43:26, "Put me in remembrance, let us plead and argue together."
   Also knowing and using God's word is where your power is coming from.
   Eph 6:17 Take the helmet of salvation and the sword of the Spirit, WHICH IS THE WORD OF GOD!

What are you going to get when we pray and I lay hands on you?

Or if you go to God direct to accept your healing? Grace!

Grace is the power of God. And it is delivered by the Holy Spirit. It is God's gift to us. It allows us to do things or have things we are incapable of having or doing.

Eph. 2:8, For it is by grace you have been saved through faith. And this is not from yourselves it is a gift of God. Paul here is not only speaking of salvation but also of healing.... Because healing is also part of the Redemption Package. (The work of Christ.) **2 Peter 2:24 By His strips we were healed.**

Jesus has given it to you... Now it is up to you to accept it... It takes the same faith to be saved as to be healed... So if you are saved, you have it... USE IT!!!!!

Here is a healing prayer that I used as I started walking with Jesus. This is a prayer I prayed in my early ministry and still use it on occasion with success. This prayer fits most baby Christians. (You can be a baby Christian a long time if you never study the word.) It is a good prayer but as you grow you will learn more.

Dear Heavenly Father. Forgive me of my sins. I know my greatest sin, is not putting you first in my life. I know how much you love me. You sent your only Son to die on the cross for me so that I might have eternal life and live with you forever. I know Jesus was whipped and by his stripes he took all of my diseases. I know you never meant for me to be ill, that all You have for me is good and positive and loving. That sickness and doubt and the

negative influences in my life are from the Devil, trying to keep me from your love. I use the name of Jesus now to loose this evil disease and cast it out of my body. I want the Devil out of my life, and I want to live my life for your glory. I want to open my heart for you to come and live inside me and guide me. Dear God, I want the healing Jesus promised. I want you to make my body whole and strong and take all the disease out of me. Help me never to doubt your word and when I read it, help me to understand what you want me to do. Dear Father, I love you so much, help me be of service to you. <u>Mark 11:24 says "Therefore I tell you, whatever you ask for in prayer, believe that you have received it, and it will be yours."</u> Dear Father, I believe your word and I believe I have received my healing. I thank you for your grace and mercy. I thank you for Jesus Christ, and thank you for healing me. I pray in Jesus precious name. Amen.

I used this prayer on Charlie Gall.

-----------------Charlie Gall-----------------

A Minister, asked me to see a friend of his and to pray for him. His name was Charlie Gall. He was about 70 and had severe heart problems. I went to the hospital and met with Charlie. We had just started talking when a friend of his came to visit. He said he would come back and I said that it was alright we would be praying and he could join us.

I started telling Charlie about Jesus and healing. Then I ask Charlie what he did. He said he was a Minister. I said, "Here I am telling you about Jesus. Let's you and I just pray and I will leave and you can visit your friend." He said "No, I want to hear about everything." So I told him everything that I knew at that time. You see it is always good to hear God's word. Even if you know it, sometimes you can not see the forest for the trees. Then we prayed. As we prayed the power of the Holy Spirit came over me like a coat.

After we prayed I held Charlie's hand to say goodbye. Tears started coming to my eyes as I told Charlie how much I loved him. I had never loved any one so much in my life. I told him he was healed. Tears were also coming from Charlie. All the way home I replayed that scene in my mind. I had just met Charlie. I did not really even know him. Why did I have this feeling? Then I knew, it was Jesus, using me, telling Charlie he was healed and that He loved him. Thank you Jesus for using me.

A month later Charlie called me up. Jesus had completely cured him and he invited me to one of his services. He also said, "By the way the friend that was in the room, he had ulcers so bad that he had not been able to work in months. He was instantly cured as he listen to us and has been back to work ever since." Praise God! Thank you Jesus!

This was the first time I had felt God's presence as I was administering His Healing Power. It felt like I was wearing a coat. The Holy Spirit was wrapped around me.

I was starting to learn how much authority Jesus had given me and how to Receive this Power!

We will get into this more in Chapter # 3 Advanced Healing, but for now I will tell you that the **Power of Jesus is Love**. When you are filled with the Power of Jesus, you are filled with God's love. You then have full authority to use His name. What is in the Name of Jesus? **Phil 2:9-10 Therefore God exalted him to the highest place and gave him the <u>name that is above every name</u>, that at the name of Jesus every knee should bow, in heaven and on earth and under the earth,**

<u>**The name above every name**</u><u>... Does Cancer or</u>
<u>Heart Disease have a name?</u>

<u>YES! They have to bow to Jesus!</u>

Now I use what the Lord has given me. His Love, His Name, His Authority. And the Power of the Holy Spirit!

I do not want to frighten a patient, when I pray so I tell them the following.

Mark 16:17 says: They will speak in other tongues. They will lay hands on the sick and they will recover. So I will tell them that I will be saying some words in the Spirit as The Holy Spirit knows things about your illness that I do not. **Romans 8:26, Likewise the Spirit also helps our infirmities. For we know not what to pray.** But The Holy Spirit does... He will guide me and pray properly for the situation.

Then I will say a few words in tongues so they will know what to expect.

1 Cor. 14:2, Anyone who speaks in tongues does not speak to man but to God..

Commanding the Disease out!

Cancer you vile creature of the Devil. I curse you and command you to shrivel up and die, in the name of Jesus. In Jesus name I command you to leave this body. You have no authority to be here. Romans 6:14, Sin shall have no dominion over a born again Christian. For (he or she) is not under law but under grace... So Satan you can no longer put disease on this body. I loose you and cast you out in the name of Jesus...... And I claim what is rightfully ours. 1 Peter 2:24, By His strips we were healed. In the name of Jesus Christ.... Be Healed.... Thank you Jesus..........

Next, I pray in the Spirit, in case the Holy Spirit wants to add something to my prayer. Many times He does....

Then I praise God. Dear Father, thank you for healing, (name). Thank you for the power and authority we have been given in Jesus' name. Thank you for your love and mercy. Thank you for Jesus and the work that He did to deliver us from sin and disease. We praise you and worship you in the name of Jesus...

Now keep praising God until your healing manifests itself physically. Then start telling the world. **Jesus is King! Jesus is my Savior, my Healer!**

Summary

1) Say it. Confess that you are going to be healed by Jesus.
2) Do it. Take action. Look for the scriptures that promise your healing, use them!
3) Use the power that Jesus has given you. Cast out the sickness...
4) Receive it. Grab hold of your healing in faith and claim it.
(Agree with God's word, not what your body says.)
(Physical healing will follow)
5) Tell it. Confess it, so others may believe.

**Do not stop people from seeing a doctor.
Unless you are sure of the level of faith they have.**

Some people might could heal a cold, but not have faith for a cancer. So if they do not have the faith, a Doctor might keep them alive long enough for them to build it. If you are seeing a Doctor now you do not have to stop. The Doctor is not healing you God is. At all of my major illnesses I consulted Doctors. However they did not cure me, God did. Some of my Doctors still can't believe what happened to me. But to their amazement they saw clogged up diseased arteries open up. Or when I had cancer it just disappeared. **They were stupefied, but I wasn't. It was just an everyday occurrence for our Lord, Jesus Christ**.

Do not let the Doctor's words lead you astray. Keep your eyes on Jesus. Romans 3:4 Let God's word be true and every man be a liar.

-----------------Acute Pancreanitis--------------

About eight years ago I had terrible pains in my chest. I thought something had burst on the inside. I was crying in pain and Beverly called an ambulance before I could even start praying. I was taken to the hospital and I was praying on the way over. When I got there I was out of pain. However they ran several tests. My enzymes were over 3000 and they should be 65. They said I had Acute Pancreanitus and put me in a room for the night. In the morning a Doctor came in and said that overnight my enzymes had drooped down to 1000. I said that was great, Jesus had healed me. At 10:00 AM a pastor friend came in and prayed with me. I did not have a pain, I felt great.

At 3:30 the Doctor came back in. He said my enzymes were back to normal and it would be a perfect time for the operation and that he had scheduled for 5:30. Just two hours away. I told him I did not need an operation Jesus had healed me. He said, "Do you want to know what is going to happen?" Yes, what's going to happen? He said, "In two hours you are going to have the operation... Or you are going to be very ill and in pain for the next six weeks and then you are going to die. "Unless, (he said, real smart), your God heals you." I said, "Well I am not having the operation." I knew that I did not want that man touching me. So check me out... He said, "I will not! And left."

I called another Doctor who was a friend of mine and said check me out of here. In a minute my Hospital Doctor was paged to the phone on the loud speaker and then he came in and tossed my chart at me and said you are checked out.... Then a nurse came in with a stack of papers for me to sign. All saying that I would die with my condition and that the hospital had no responsibility for my death. I had to sign all of these to get out. Which I did, and I got out.

I felt great until the next day at lunch. I ate and then the pain came back. And I heard the doctor say you will be sick for six weeks and then you will die. I cursed the pain and commanded it to leave. It did. This repeated itself at every meal for the next three days. At which time, I quit cussing the Devil and cussed myself out.

I said, Ferd, "Who are you going to believe? Jesus, who has cured you of heart disease... Healed you of cancer... Healed you of a stroke... Has called you by name... Has come to you in a vision. Who is your Savior. Your constant companion. The love of your life. Or the atheist Doctor." The choice was easy. Jesus' words were true.... let every man be a liar. I confessed that and to this day have not had another pain. **Thank you Jesus.**

This is to show you that no matter how strong you think you are, you can still be had...The Devil will keep trying to take you down. And if you do not keep your eye on Jesus he will do it.

Say this aloud:

I am fully persuaded that what God's word says....

He is able to do!

I am fully persuaded that what God's word says....

He is able to do!

Praise you Father...Thank you Jesus...

Eph 3:20-21
Now to him who is able to do immeasurably more than all we ask or imagine, according to his power that is at work within us, to him be glory in the Church and in Christ Jesus throughout all generations, for ever and ever! Amen.

Chapter 4

Advanced: Know who you are in Christ

Most Christians do not know who they are! What they possess! Or what God intends for them to do with it! We usually look at ourselves as man sees us. How does God see us? This gave me a big revaluation of my life. I was always afraid that I was over stepping my authority. I did not want to seem presumptuous.... Was I ordained to do this?????
Then Jesus led me to see who I was in Him

Eph. 2:6, God has raised us up together with Christ.
In God's eyes you are seated with Jesus at His right hand. You are in Christ, just as Christ is in you here on earth.

1Cor. 6:17, He that is joined to the Lord is one spirit.
You and Jesus could be no closer together. Jesus is not just with you, you are part of each other. Think about that... You are one spirit with Christ. If you believe that, than when you lay hands on someone. It is not just you, it is you and Jesus. That is where your power is coming from.

1Cor. 12:27, Now you are the body of Christ.
What does that mean? We Christians here on earth are the body of Christ. He is the Head, we are the body. The head does the thinking and the leading, and the body carries out the work.

So when Jesus wants something done here on earth it is up to us to do it. How could we? Easy, with Jesus' Spirit joined to ours He is transferring His authority and power to us to do His will. But we must except it and be obedient to His commands,

If God is depending on you, is He in trouble? Are you following His commands?

Matt. 28:20, "And I am always with you."
All power belongs to Jesus.... and Jesus is always with us. So we have that power in us at all times.

Eph. 3:20, His power is at work in us.
His power is not dormant! It is at work. That means we are, or should be using it. How many of us are really using it? Isn't it time we realized what Jesus has done for us and start doing what He intended. Being His body here on Earth!

HOW MUCH POWER IS THAT?
Matt. 28:18, Jesus said, "All power is given to me in Heaven and Earth."

Eph. 11:19-20, His power is like He used to raise Jesus.

Jesus', Divine Authority Has Been Transferred to Us!

Acts 1:8, "You shall receive power after the Holy Spirit has come upon you."

Matt 16:19 I will give you the keys of the kingdom of heaven; whatever you bind on earth will be bound in heaven and whatever you loose on earth will be loosed in heaven."

Mark 16:17, In my name, they will drive out demons..... They will place hands on the sick and they will get well...

Luke 10:19, "I have given you authority to trample on snakes and scorpions (Devils and Demons) and to overcome all the power of the enemy; nothing will harm you."

Mark 9:23, Jesus said, "Everything is possible for him who believes."

John 15:7, Jesus said, "<u>If you will remain In my words..</u> Whatever you ask will be given to you."

1 John 4:4, Greater is He that is in you than He that is in the world.

Eph. 2:10, For we are God's workmanship, created in Jesus Christ, to do good works, which God prepared in advance for us to do.
   ___*Now check this one out!!!!*___   John 14:12 Jesus said, "I tell you the truth, anyone who has faith in me will do what I have been doing. He will do even greater things than these....
   So if we can believe, Jesus, gives us all the power that we can believe for.

That is the power to raise the dead. That is the power to heal the sick. That is the power to trample the Devil and all evil forces that come against us. That is the power to be the Body of Christ.

How to get Super Power! John 17:22, I have given <u>them</u> the Glory, that you gave me, that <u>they</u> may be one as we are one. <u>Them! They! That is us the body of Christ.</u>

If we unite as the body of Christ we have Corporate Power... Dynamic Power!

THAT IS THE POWER OF GOD!   THANK YOU JESUS.... But you can only use a gift that you know you have, and that you accept. And we can only use it through Jesus, because of God's grace and love for us.
And the filling of His love is the Ultimate Power.

------------------Brother Big Boy-----------------

This will show you what corporate power can do, if you will just believe. In 1999 we were having a Church dinner after the Service. The women were all outside in the yard getting the food ready. Several of us were still in the Church. We heard a body fall to the floor. We went over to see who it was. It was Brother Big Boy, a member about 70 years old. He lay beside the pews, dead. One of the women was a nurse. She went to her car and got a stethoscope. She checked him and the Pastor did also. Brother Big Boy was dead.

More people had heard and were coming in from outside. Probably five minutes had already passed. Now the ones closest to Big Boy laid hands on him. The others stood over him with their hands stretched out. Then we prayed. Some, in the Spirit. Some, in the natural. We prayed for fifteen minutes. Brother Big Boy had been dead now for twenty minutes, then suddenly he twitched. Then he opened his eyes. We sat him back up in a chair and he said, "I think I just need to catch my breath." Well I guess he did. He then went out and had lunch with us, and had a wonderful time.

Several months went by and I was telling the story to a friend when it just dawned on me... When it happened, no one in the whole congregation thought about giving him CPR. No one thought about calling an ambulance to get him to the hospital. We went directly to prayer. It was just like the most natural thing in the world that we should have done.

Last Sunday I was in Church with Brother Big Boy. He takes up the collection for us... And he never misses a service. Well something strange happened after he came back to us. He looks ten years younger. His heart never hurts any more and he just glows with the love of Jesus. Of course he should, he got to meet Him, personally.

"Beloved, now we are the sons of God" 1 John 3:2

If sonship, heirship; if heirs, then joint heirs... Look at the tremendous power and love God has given us. To be His Son or Daughter, to share His power.

Dare you believe and take hold of this gift. That is what Jesus wants you to have.

Sons of God speak and it is done... Matt. 16:19, They may bind things that are loose, and loose things that are bound.... 1 John 4:17, "As He is, so are we in this world." Who dares to believe it? Oh, what would happen if we learned the secret.... to ask once and believe?

How do you use this power that Jesus has given us?

First, we have to stop looking at things in the natural... Man looks at the situation, tries to work the problem out with his ability, gets into a corner and cannot get out. Then starts praying. HELP ME.....HELP ME! Then, waits for God to answer his prayer. If God does not, then he says God does not love me. I am not worthy. Or worse, I do not have faith in God. While God, all the time is looking at you, A Christian... A Bible carrying Christian... **And God asks, "What is the matter with you now? I have given you everything you need, even the Spirit of my Son, with all the power of God... And you sit there crying."**

If your son came crying to you and said Dad, The car you gave me will not start.... **(God's gifts to you do not work.)** You would say why? He says, "I do not know." "Did you try to start it?" "No." "Why not?" "I did not know how." "Well did you read the instruction book I gave you?" **(The Bible.)** "Well I looked at it." "Have you tried the key?" **(Faith)** He proudly shows his Dad the key which is on a necklace around his neck. "Oh I carry that around with me all the time." Dad said, "well put it in the lock and turn it. And do not bother me again until you read the book and know what you are doing."

Thankfully our Father God has more patience with us than our natural fathers, or we would all be dead from our stupidity. But some very powerful men in God have made this same mistake.

------------------Moses------------------

God commanded Moses to lead His people out of Egypt. **And gave Moses a staff that was to represent God's power and authority to be used when needed**. This worked fine until they were trapped at the Red Sea. The Egyptians were at the rear and Mountains on each side.   Moses started to pray. We do not know what he said but it was probably something like, "Oh God get us out of here. I've done everything you have asked and now look at the mess I have made. HELP!"

Well we know what God said. **Exodus 14:15-16, The Lord said to Moses, "Why cry to me? Speak to the children of Israel, that they go forward: Just lift up your rod and stretch out your hand over the sea, and divide it......"**

Why was God impatient with Moses? He said, **"Why cry to me!"** Because He had given Moses His power and authority to get the job done and he was not using it.

Through Jesus, we have been given God's power and authority. <u>Are we using it?</u>

We have even more than Moses had. We have Jesus, as our intercessor and The Holy Spirit living on the inside of us....

God demands the action of the believer's faith.. Stretch out your hands and divide the water... God has given every believer (Romans 12:3) "The Measure of Faith" (the rod) and it is for man, as Jesus' body here on earth, to use it... And even more, He has given the Spirit of his Son to us, to show us the way. And to be as a seal, (Eph. 1:13) to show the Devil who we are, Sons of God!!!! With The Authority of God Almighty!!!!

We do not have to beg for what is ours. No, we go out in the name of Jesus as Kings here on Earth. Jesus has given us power to tread on scorpions and snakes. (evil spirits) To heal the sick. And to use His name. And Nothing Will Harm Us! Mark 16:17 and Luke 10:19   Thank You Jesus!

But! To know is not enough.... We must do it!

James 1:22, But, be you doers of the word, and not hearers only.

Over and over in the New Testament the Word of God says, "They healed them." The Disciples healed them. **And I did not see anyone praying to get it done.** When Peter and John saw the cripple at the Gate Beautiful, they used the rod of God. **(Their Faith)** They did not pray, they commanded. **"In the name of Jesus Christ of Nazareth rise up and walk." Acts 3:6** And the man got up and walked.

The power of Jesus name, with their faith, that made him walk!

We have this power. And do not ever think that the Devil does not know who we are and what we have. **2 Cor. 1:22, God set His seal of ownership upon us.** But the Devil, will try to scare you and push you as far as he can. **Until you say STOP!** He's like the school yard bully... He will push until you say, **I'm fighting back! Devil you will have to whip me, and then my Brother Jesus, and then my Father God!!!** Let me tell you he has been against them before and he wants no part of them. So when he knows that you have their authority behind you... **End of fight!!!**

God loves us so dearly. Psalm 8:4-6, David said, "What is man, that you are mindful of him? And the son of man, that you visit him? For you made him a little lower than the angels, and have crowned him with glory and honor. You made him to have dominion over the works of your hands; <u>you have put all things under his feet.</u>"

We will never know how much God loves us. But we can try to show our love and our gratitude, by being the best that we can be, by using what He has given us, His Glory and to Glorify His Son, Jesus, who gave everything for us and to us.

THANK YOU FATHER. THANK YOU JESUS.

Let us look at John 14:12-14 again!

12 Verily, verily, I say unto you, He that believeth on me, <u>the works that I do shall he do also; and greater works than these shall he do;</u> because I go unto my Father.

13 And <u>whatsoever ye shall ask in my name, that will I do,</u> that the Father may be glorified in the Son.

14 If ye shall <u>ask any thing in my name, I will do it.</u>

You have just learned who you are in Christ. Jesus has given us His Power and Authority, use it... You will notice in the Bible that Jesus never prayed for anyone. His disciples never prayed for anyone, we are speaking only of healing... Like, "Pick up your bed and go. Or like Peter and John who said, "In the name of Jesus, rise and walk. They commanded. **You too can command!**

If you believe in your heart, this will work! Be careful... You might start thinking you are doing this. **Rom 12:3 3 For I say, through the grace given unto me, to every man that is among you, not to think of himself more highly than he ought to think; but to think soberly, according as God hath dealt to every man the measure of faith.**

You see, you are not special; God has given all of us this ability if we can believe it. However, you are only a part of healing. Jesus is the biggest part. You are nothing without Him. If you start going over the line, Jesus will let you know. That is a serious wake up call.

You have a part to play and Jesus has a part to play. Jesus made that very clear to me...

------------Jesus cuts me down to size!-----------

After starting 2jesus, many people were coming for healing and many were also getting healed. I was trying so hard. I worried about everyone. I did not want to let Jesus down, I owed Him my life. I felt it was up to me to get these people healed. Did I say the right thing? Was there anything else I could have done? I was worrying constantly. I was making myself sick; my wife said that I had to stop. I told her I could not. I had to do this for Jesus.
        (Do you see how many times I said I)

Then Jesus, called my name. **He said "Ferd, who do you think you are? You give them the word, I heal them."** You see, I was trying to do everything. I said, "Thank you." And I never worried again. I knew now the part that I was to play. I was trying to do my part and His too. I could not... So Jesus straightened me out. I give them the word and Jesus takes over and heals them. Thanks you Jesus!
Now I am trying to give you all the things that I know about Jesus and healing. I want you to have this power and authority, down in your heart. I want you to believe that Jesus is who He says He is and that His promises are for you.
My job is to build your faith in Jesus and His Word. I will be here to help you pray..... But then I am going to turn you over to Jesus. Jesus, will then put the power to His Words and you will be healed in the name of Jesus. Praise God!

Chapter 5

Advanced: Doubt, the Devils Best Weapon

What is Webster's definition of doubt?

To waiver in opinion. Someone who is not consistent. Unsettled in opinion or belief. Inclined to disbelieve. Fearful, Apprehensive or Suspicious of.

Do you see yourself in one of the words above? If so you may have the answer to why your prayers or commands are not getting answered. All Christians have doubts from time to time. It is the strongest weapon that the Devil has. Because with doubt he can cripple you, because when doubt comes, fear comes, and with fear, faith leaves. Without faith Jesus can no longer help you.

But let him ask in faith, nothing wavering. For he that wavers is like a wave of the sea driven with the wind and tossed. For let not that man think that he shall receive anything of the Lord. (James 1:6-7)

Where does this doubt come from? Reasoning. What is reasoning?

Reasoning is the cognitive process of looking for reasons, beliefs, conclusions, actions or feelings. The process of using your mind to consider something carefully; course of reasoning aimed at demonstrating a truth or falsehood; the methodical process of logical reasoning;

We do this all the time. We use human logic to analyze everything we are doing. This works in the natural system of the world. (And that system is controlled by the Devil.) We use this daily with natural problems.

Matt 4:8-9
8   Again, the devil took Jesus, to a very high mountain and showed him all the kingdoms of the world and their splendor.
9 "All this I will give you," he said, "if you will bow down and worship me."

So you see, we live in the Devil's world. It uses, lust, greed, power and worldly knowledge. However for Divine Healing, we will be moving and believing in the Spiritual system. In God's Domain.

You do not reason with God's Word. That would be wavering in belief. God's word is absolute truth. So you do not have to try to make it line up with human knowledge. It will not. And that is why many are not healed. They want to believe, but find that they can not.

1 Cor 1:19-21
19 For it is written: "I will destroy the wisdom of the wise; the intelligence of the intelligent I will frustrate."
20 Where is the wise man? Where is the scholar? Where is the philosopher of this age? Has not God made foolish the wisdom of the world?
21 For since in the wisdom of God the world through its wisdom did not know him, God was pleased

through the foolishness of what was preached to save those who believe. (Can you believe? If so you can be healed.)

Ps 119:160 God's word is true from the beginning: and every one of His righteous judgments endures for ever.

John 8:31-32
31 Jesus said, "If you hold to my teaching, you are really my disciples.
32 Then you will know the truth, and the truth will set you free."

John 16:13-15
13 But when He, the Spirit of truth, comes, (Upon You) He will guide you into all truth. He will not speak on his own; He will speak only what He hears, (and He hears only from Jesus) and He will tell you what is yet to come.
14 He will bring glory to Me, (Jesus) by taking from what is mine and making it known to you.
15 All that belongs to the Father is mine. That is why I said the Spirit will take from what is mine and make it known to you.

Now do you really realize what Jesus just told you? If you have the Holy Spirit in you, you have the knowledge of God. It will then be clear that God's word is the real truth.

So what are we going to do to combat doubt?

Who are we fighting? The Devil, he puts in thoughts of doubt. How to fight!

2 Cor 10:3-5
3 For though we walk in the flesh, we do not war after the flesh:
4 (For the weapons of our warfare are not carnal, but mighty through God to the pulling down of strong holds;)
5 Casting down imaginations, and every high thing that exalts itself against the knowledge of God, and bringing into captivity every thought to the obedience of Christ;

Eph. 6:14-18 The Armor of God, Belt of Truth, Breast Plate of Righteousness, Feet fitted with the Gospel of Peace, Shield of Faith, The Helmet of Salvation, Sword of the Spirit, which is the Word of God...

These are all defensive weapons except one. **The Sword, which is the Word of God.** Jesus fought with the word. He would say, "It is written!" There is also one more weapon that is an offensive weapon. Look at verse **18... Pray in the Spirit on all occasions.** That is when our Commander and Chief directs our path. He, charges His Angels to watch over us and to destroy our enemies. If you do not speak in the Spirit yet, earnestly desire this gift.

We are going to keep our eyes on Jesus. As a creature of this world all we have ever experienced before we became a Christian was the natural, or the world around us. The Bible, says that the world belongs to the Devil and he is constantly trying to keep us away from the Lord. But with Jesus you are stronger than the world. **Jesus said, "These things I have spoken to you, that in Me you might have peace. In the world you shall have tribulation: but be of good cheer; I have overcome the world." (John 16:33)**

-----------------**Jesus & Peter**---------------

Let us look at a passage where Jesus and Peter confront doubt.

(Matthew 14:25-31) 25) During the fourth watch of the night, Jesus went out to them, walking on the lake. 26) When the disciples saw Him walking on the lake, they were terrified. "It's a ghost" they said and cried out in fear. 27) But Jesus immediately said to them: Take courage! It is I, don't be afraid. 28) "Lord if its you," Peter replied, "tell me to come to you on the water." 29) "Come," He said. Then Peter got down out of the boat, walked on the water and came toward Jesus. 30) But when he saw the wind, he was afraid and, beginning to sink cried out, "Lord save me." 31) Immediately Jesus reached out His hand and caught him. "You of little faith," He said, "why did you doubt?"

Peter was in trouble right from the get go. **28) "Lord if its you," Peter replied,** Peter had been with the Lord for three years and he is starting to doubt. "Is that you?" And Jesus replied "It is I". Jesus was somewhere Peter did not expect Him to be. Walking on the water. We are going to have to know Jesus well enough to know Him when He is talking to us. So to do that we have to spend time with Him. But just like Peter we can be fooled, if we find Jesus somewhere that we think He is not suppose to be. When we ask Jesus if we can come to Him sometimes we are going to have to be ready to follow Jesus even into the water. Peter did. **Peter replied, "Tell me to come to you on the water."** Now is where the rubber meets the road. When we are following Jesus we must have faith that what He tells us is right. No matter what the natural circumstances are. Simply we must keep our eyes on Jesus and His words. Let's watch Peter. **"Come," He said. Then Peter got down out of the boat, walked on the water and came toward Jesus.** He walked on the water. He walked on the water. Peter walked on the water! Does that give you any idea what we are capable of if, We have faith in Jesus? But here comes the rub. **30) But when he saw the wind, he was afraid and, beginning to sink crying out, "Lord save me."** Peter took his eyes off Jesus and looked at the natural. He saw the wind and the waves and became afraid, and with fear, faith leaves. But notice Peter began to sink. He had time to call to Jesus and Jesus had time to pick him up. So he had some faith left. **31) Immediately Jesus reached out His hand and caught him. "You of little faith," He said, "why did you doubt?"** Jesus didn't say Peter had no faith. He said "You of little faith why did you doubt?"

    I think that here is one of the greatest lessons in the Bible. As we are sinking with heart disease or cancer, if we have little faith and call out to Jesus, He will be there.

PRAISE GOD----THANK YOU JESUS-----GLORY---GLORY---GLORY

Even when our faith is weak Jesus will save us if we call out to Him. You must keep your eyes on Gods unchanging word, no matter what the circumstances are. God through Jesus Christ and The Holy Spirit are greater than the circumstances. But if you allow the circumstances to control you, you are going to sink.

Jesus said, "These things I have spoken to you, that in Me, you might have peace. In the world, you shall have tribulation: but be of good cheer; I have overcome the world."   (John 16:33)
Let us look at how doubt can kill..........

--------------Jim------------

I was asked by a friend to see a man that was a terminal cancer patient. He was in his late 50's. He had smoked all of his life and had cancer all over his body. They had cut away part of his throat and some of his cheeks. It gave him a funny high voice. He had been a construction worker with a good build, but now weighed about 90 pounds. The hospital had turned him out to die. I asked if I could tell him about Jesus and how Jesus healed. He said yes he would like that.

I went over with Jim what I had learned about Jesus and what Jesus had done for me. We spent the better part of an afternoon together. Jim was soaking it up like a sponge. Maryland, his wife was also listening carefully. At the end we prayed.

As I took my hands off Jim, he jumped straight up and yelled, "I'm healed." He said that he was always in continual pain and that it was gone. **Praise God!**

Jim and I started meeting for lunch everyday. When I would come into the restaurant, Jim would smile with a thumbs up and say praise the Lord. This went on for about five months. Everything was great. No pain, gaining weight, and happy. Then one day I came in and Jim did not look good. He said he was in great pain. He was holding his side and said that it was his kidneys. He said, the cancer had returned. I tried to cheer him up, but I did not do a good job. We tried to pray but his heart was not in it.

The next day I came in and Jim ask me to go outside with him. He said, "Ferd, the pain is so bad I cannot stand it. I have been praying that I would die. Would you also pray that I would die." I said, I would not pray that he would die. But I would pray that he would be out of pain. That was the last time I saw Jim. I left the next day on a cruise, and stayed away ten days. When I came back I went to the restaurant and Jim was not there. They said he had died right after I left and that he had already been buried. What had happened? I thought he had been healed. It saddens me when people I love cannot get God's best. Was he ever healed?

Three months later his wife Maryland called. She said that she was cleaning out Jim's billfold and found my card and there was something she thought I would like to know. Jim, was in a law suit against one of the hospitals for wrong treatments of some kind and when he died they had to do an autopsy for the case. <u>She said, "Ferd, there was not one cancer cell in his body. All of his organs were perfect."</u> He had died of a heart attack." I told Maryland thank you. Then I told God, thank you. He had done as He said He would. God had healed Jim. Then I thanked God for the autopsy. That I had proof of His word. I told the people at the restaurant, who had been praising his healing, that when God heals, you are healed. So what happened? The Devil had put a seed of doubt in Jim and it grew. The Devil gave him pain. And fear came and it was a vicious cycle of pain and fear, until his heart could not stand it anymore and burst.

I'm telling you this story, because if you are a healer or a patient. And God heals you. You are healed. But you must grab hold tight and not let the Devil fool you into believing otherwise. The Devil will fight you every step of the way and you must use all of the weapons Jesus has given you to survive in this world.

How do you get Doubt out? You command it out in the name of Jesus.

"Doubt, you demon from hell. I command you out in the name of Jesus. This body, mind and spirit belong to Jesus and you have no control over it. In Jesus name out!"

Then keep your eyes and mind on Jesus.

You have the power and authority

To do what Jesus says you can do!

Thank you Jesus!

Chapter 6

Advanced: Faith Your Life Line to God

What it is and how it works.

1) Faith and Belief:

Most people think faith and belief are the same thing. WRONG! You can believe something and not have faith in it.

A man staggers up to you he is dying of starvation. You put food in front of him, he just looks at it. You say this food will nourish you and keep you alive, do you believe that? Yes, I believe that. The man just looks at it and then he dies. Why did he die? Because he did not eat the food. The eating of the food is faith. **Faith is acting on what you believe**. Many Christians today believe in the Bible; they believe all of God's promises. However if they don't have faith and act on the word of God they will not receive all of Gods best that He wants them to have. If they don't have faith they will die just like our man died. They will be sick but not get God's healing. They won't have God's prosperity. They won't have God's peace and contentment. And the worst part is they will never please God without faith. *Without faith you can't please God. [Hebrews 11:6]*

You have to do more than just believe. You have to act on what you believe!

You have to act on God's word! And that action is what faith is. The word of God works when you do what it says.

<u>SAY ALOUD...........</u>
<u>The word of God works.. When you do what it says..</u>

2) Faith, in the spirit realm and natural realm:
Faith is the same in the spirit realm as it is in the natural realm. The spiritual realm is God's realm. The natural realm is Satan's realm. However faith works the same in either realm. Here's how faith works in the natural realm. 1) You are given information. 2) You believe that information. 3) You act on it. (The acting is faith.)

Example: You went to get a job, and were hired at $5.00 per hour. The boss said that you would get paid on Friday. So you worked all week believing the man would pay you. Working that week was faith <u>you acted on what he said.</u> You believed what the man said. A man you never knew before said he would pay you on Friday. You worked (acted) on faith.

But, when it comes from God you have to have a sign or someone to prophesy over you to confirm that the Lord meant what he said, when He said it. The word of a man you will swallow hook line and sinker, but from God who created you, and the universe, who gave you the greatest instruction book the world has ever known, the Bible, <u>YOU WANT A SIGN before you will act on his word.</u>

You can be sick in the hospital. The Doctor comes in and says you are doing fine you will be home in three days. When your relatives come in you say, "I'm doing fine, I'm going home in three days." You still have the pain but now know you are getting well. But when it comes to God you still say you're sick even though *His word says that by His strips you are healed. (I Peter 2:24)*

You say you believe His word. But if you are not acting on it, God's word will never do you any personal good.

You have an automobile; you have the key in your pocket. You can believe that key will start your car, and it will. You can believe that the car will take you home, and it will. But it will never start the car or take you home until you put the key in the lock and turn it on. **God's word is the key. You can believe His word is the key. But until you act on it and put it into the lock of life, into the circumstances of life, it will never do you any good.**

3) Faith is the evidence of God's promises.

Now faith is the substance of things hoped for, the evidence of things not seen. (Hebrews 11 : 1)

If faith is the evidence, then the thing although not seen, must be real. You can't have evidence for something that doesn't exist. So faith is the evidence of things not seen.

What does evidence mean? Evidence is that which supports the existence of something. The fact that something exists, something that you're unable to see, you need the evidence to prove it. *(II Corinthians 4:18) While we look not at things which are seen, but at things which are not seen:*

for the _things_ which are seen are temporal; but the _things_ which are not seen are eternal. That sounds ridiculous. How can you look at something that is not seen?

Only with the eye of faith.

As Christians we must live our lives by faith. **(II Corinthians 5 : 7) For we walk by faith, not by sight:** That means the man of God walks by faith. He doesn't walk by what he sees. He bases his action on the word of God. That is why it is so important to know what the word of God says. God's word says, **"While we look not at the things that are seen, but at things that are not seen."** Don't look at the cancer or heart disease in the natural. Look at them through God's words. **"Himself took our infirmities, and bare our sickness" (Matthew 8 : 17).** Why did He bare them if He wants us to bare them?

(I Peter 2 : 24) "by whose stripes you were healed" YOU WERE HEALED, not going to be, you are! You might say, well how come I'm sick? Because you are saying you are sick. The word of God says you are well. But as long as you take sides against the word of God, the word of God can not work on your behalf.

When you get in line with the word, **by his stripes I was healed,** sickness and disease will flee. It will not be able to stay there. (But you have to believe that in your heart.)

Acting on God's word will bring the evidence of things hoped for, (our healing, or whatever blessing you are in need of,) into the natural world. As Jesus said over and over again to the people

He healed, **"Your faith has made you whole."** Jesus, took spiritual gifts from the spirit world into the natural world.

Jesus blessed us with all spiritual blessings. ***(Ephesians 1:3) Blessed be the God and Father of our Lord Jesus Christ, <u>who has blessed us with all spiritual blessings </u>in heavenly places in Christ:*** <u>Not some but all spiritual blessings</u>, and FAITH is our blank check to draw on these blessings to give us life and give it more abundantly. So with faith we can bring <u>things</u> from the spirit world into the natural world.

SAY ALOUD...
(Hebrew 11 : 1) **Now faith is the substance of <u>things</u> hoped for, the evidence of <u>things</u> not seen. Thank you Jesus.**

4) Things you can't see are real.

Everything material was first of all spiritual before God made it into the physical. It existed first in the mind of God before it was produced in physical manifestation. Since everything was first of all spiritual, spiritual things are more real than physical things. Just because you can't see it or feel it doesn't mean it doesn't exist.

At this very moment the air is full of FM and AM radio waves, also UHF and VHF television pictures. But just because you can't see them or touch them doesn't mean that they are not real. You just don't have the proper apparatus to tune them in. With a TV set or radio they are perfectly clear. Faith is the TV set that tunes into the realm of God. Your Bible is your TV guide to find out what programs are on. You'll find it covers everything.

5) Faith is ....present tense
(Hebrews 11 : 1) <u>*Now*</u> *faith is the substance of things hoped for, the evidence of things not seen.* <u>**NOW faith ..IS...not yesterday.. not next week......**</u> <u>**NOW.**</u> You can't believe that God is going to heal you someday. You'll never get healed. **You have to believe you are healed right now before it will work. "Now faith is...."**

(Mark 11 : 24) *24 Therefore I say unto you, what things soever ye desire, when ye pray,* <u>*believe that*</u> <u>*ye receive them, and ye shall have them.*</u> Jesus is speaking and He is saying something very important. Therefore Jesus says unto you, what things soever you desire............things......Health or other

Promises of God.   Believe that you receive them...Received them...He didn't say feel you received them......He said when you pray <u>believe you have received them, and you shall have them!</u> When you pray ...is now....... believe you have received......is now.   and you shall have them.....is future.

If you believe Gods word**...and act on it,,(that's** **faith)...**you shall have the promise. In other words He will bring them into the physical world to you. If you don't act on His words you will not get it. **(Hebrews 4:2 But the message that they heard was of no value to them, because those who heard did not combine it with faith.)**

Now if you believe that you have received it than you will not pray for it again. Why ask God for something you already have? If you ask again it would mean you did not believe you got it the first time.... If that is what you believe than you will not get it. Faith is acting on God's word, even for things you do not see. For we walk by faith not by sight. If we act on God's word **He will fulfill the promise**. "Believe you have received them, and **you shall have them."**

Many of us are waiting for God to work a miracle or give us a healing, and then we will believe it. *(Luke 6:46) And why call ye me, Lord, Lord, and do not the things which I say?* So, you see, you have to believe you have it **NOW.**

ACT like it's true, (that's faith) and then the power of God will come. Because that's how faith works, dotting the I's and crossing the T's, following God's instructions exactly.

6) Faith is......the title deed.

A man comes to you with a great buy, five acres for $500 dollars. You haven't seen the land it is in another State, but you don't need to, you want it. So the man gives you the title deed. It is yours and you will see it later. Now faith is the title deed of the things we hope for, being the proof of things we do not see.... And that title deed is backed by the word of GOD**! The Bible says God cannot lie *(Hebrews 6:18)***

<u>*SAY ALOUD*</u>
<u>*So if He says I have it, I have it!   If He says I will receive it, I will receive it!*</u>

<u>God Can not and will not Lie!!!!!</u>

7) There are two kinds of faith...God's kind and man's kind

The man's kind of faith says, "I'll believe it when I see it.... I'll believe it when I feel it." The God's kind of faith says, "I believe it, therefore **I WILL** see it. **The God kind of faith believes first of all, and then confesses with the mouth what it believes.**

-------------------**Jesus & Fig Tree**----------------

In Mark 11, Jesus went to a fig tree to get some fruit, but the tree was bear. So He spoke to the tree. *(Mark 11:14) And Jesus said unto it, no man eat fruit of thee hereafter forever. And His disciples heard it.* Jesus was born and raised in this part of the country, He knew when fig trees had figs, He was trying to teach his disciples a lesson. For *(Mark 11:14) says, and His disciples heard it.*   The next day as they passed by Peter looked at the tree and it had withered away. So they asked Jesus about it. *(Mark 11:22-24) 22 And Jesus said unto them. Have faith in God (or the God kind of faith) 23 For verily I say unto you, That whosoever shall say unto this mountain, Be thou removed, and be thou cast into the sea; and shall not doubt in his heart, but shall believe that those things which he says shall come to pass; he shall have whatever he says. 24 Therefore I say* *unto you, **What things soever you desire, when you pray, believe that you receive them, and you shall have them.***

Concerning the fig tree: His disciples heard Him. Jesus was not afraid to commit Himself. He spoke out loud. **<u>He confessed with His mouth what He believed in His heart</u>.** He believed when He spoke that the tree would obey Him. It would dry up. And He dared to speak it...... Do you have that kind of faith in the word of God? **Do you believe when you tell a fever to go that it is going to leave?** Do you believe when you say that my needs are met in Jesus Christ, that they are met? The God kind of faith does. It believes in the heart and **confesses with the mouth**. It shows that you are committed to the word of God. **And that you WILL ACT on His word.**

The God kind of faith believes it, and says it, without seeing anything.... That tree didn't dry up for 24 hours. It wasn't until the next day that Peter noticed that the tree had dried up. Jesus spoke that word. **It was the word of faith. It was the God kind of faith.**

8) We are God's children

We are God's children so we should have the same kind of faith. The Bible says if you are born again you are a son of God. Therefore we ought to exercise the same kind of faith our Father does. All through the Bible it states, **And God said**...and when He spoke something happened. **He said "let there be light"....** and what happened? There was! Notice nothing came into being until God said it. **The God kind of faith works by believing with the heart and confessing with the mouth.**

9) How do we know we have that kind of faith?

Would you like to have the God kind of faith? The kind of faith that Jesus had? If you are a believer, if you have been born again, **You already have the God kind of faith.** "Yes but I don't feel like I have it." It has nothing to do with how you feel. It's so because God said it is so, not because you feel like it.

(Romans 12 : 3) ...according as God hath dealt to every man the measure of faith.

God dealt it to us. We must clarify that Paul didn't mean every man in the world. As he was talking to the Church in Rome He meant only the believers in Christ.

(Ephesians 2:8-9) For by grace are you saved through faith; and that not of yourselves; it is the gift of God. 9) Not of works, lest any man should boast.

You can not work to get this... it is by His grace. Romans 12:3 was how you got faith. Now how do you get more?

(Romans 10:17) So then faith comes by hearing and hearing by the word of God.

That's how it comes and the only way you'll get it. A friend of mine says if you don't go to church and never hear the word, than you had better start reading the Bible out loud.

Do you know why many people do not have divine healing, the baptism of the Holy Spirit or speaking in other tongues? It is because they don't go to church or where they go they do not preach on these subjects. So they have no faith built up for it. You only have faith for what you have heard. A lot of Christians are saved, thank God, because that is all they have heard about. That is wonderful that will get us to Heaven. But it is not going to do us a lot of good down here.

However God wants us to have LIFE and HAVE IT MORE ABUNDANTLY.

10) The God kind of faith in your heart and in your mouth.

(Matthew 12:34) out of the abundance of the heart the mouth speaks.

So get the word into your heart, keep pounding it into your brain until it gets down into your heart. (When the Bible speaks of your heart it means your spirit.)

(Mark 11 : 23) Jesus said..."whoever shall SAY unto this mountain, be thou removed and be thou cast into the sea, and shall not doubt in his heart, but shall believe that those things which he SAYS shall come to pass; he shall have whatever he SAYS.

So say it, speak it out. When you speak it out things will begin to happen on your behalf. Believing it in the heart and confessing it with your mouth. That's what Jesus did...... He believed with His heart...... He spoke it with his mouth.

Chapter 7

Advanced: The Power of the Tongue!

THE COMBINATION THAT OPENS THE LOCK.

Speaking Victory!

John 1:1-4 In the beginning was the Word, and the Word was with God, and the Word was God. 2 He was with God in the beginning. 3 Through him all things were made; without him nothing was made that has been made. 4 In him was life, and that life was the light of men.

Heb 1:3 The Son is the radiance of God's glory and the exact representation of his being, sustaining all things by his POWERFUL WORD.

There is noting more powerful than the Word of God!

God created the world by His Word. God sustains all things by His Word.

It is not impossible for God to do anything that He declares. He can speak and it will happen. And we find that He created man in His own image. We have the ability to operate in the same kind of faith.

What do we need to make this work? The knowledge of God, which is the Word of God.

When we align ourselves up with the Word of God we are bringing into our lives the power that Jesus meant for us to have. Look at this verse. Jesus is giving His word to us with all of His love and authority.

John 14:12-14, I tell you the truth, anyone who has faith in me will do what I have been doing. He will do even greater things than these, because I am going to the Father. 13 And I will do whatever you ask in my name, so that the Son may bring glory to the Father. 14 You may ask me for anything in my name, and I will do it.

Luke 10:19 I have given you authority to trample on snakes and scorpions (evil spirits) and to overcome all the power of the enemy; nothing will harm you.

When we line our lives and our words up with Jesus' Words,
WE HAVE VICTORY!

But look what James says:
James 1:26 If anyone considers himself religious and yet does not keep a tight rein on his tongue, he deceives himself and his religion is worthless.

James 3:6 The tongue also is a fire, a world of evil among the parts of the body. It corrupts the whole

person, sets the whole course of his life on fire, and is itself set on fire by hell.

Is it any wonder that we are sick, that we do not have the power that Jesus meant for us to have. James tells us that we are letting the devil control our tongue. We can not serve two masters... **We have to kick the devil out of our lives and out of our mouths!**

How are we going to do this? By filling our heart with the Word, the Word is our power. The Word gives us the knowledge of God and when we stand in agreement with God, speaking His Words, the victory is ours. The devil, and his demons, which are destroying our lives with illness and disease, corruption and sin, **Are Cast Out,** because we have filled our heart with good things. The Words of God!

Out of the abundance of the heart the mouth speaks. Matt. 12:34 You will never get good things out of your mouth if you do not abundantly put good things in your heart. So we must spend time reading and listening to God's word.

How Should We Speak?

Proverbs 18:21 The power of life and death are in the tongue.

So we speak life, health and joy! We speak positively, not negatively. We speak hope, not despair. We speak health, not sickness. We speak good, not evil. We build people up, not tear them down. We think before we open our mouth... What would Jesus say? Then we line up with His Word and say it!

How to Pray....

Prayer should always be spoken. Not thought. Our power comes by speaking God filled words. Words of Faith, Faith filled Words bring God on the scene.

Jesus said, John 16:23-24 In that day you will no longer <u>ask</u> me anything. I tell you the truth, my Father will give you whatever you <u>ask</u> in my name. 24 Until now you have not <u>asked</u> for anything in my name. <u>Ask</u> and you will receive, and your joy will be complete.

Mark 11:23-24 "I tell you the truth, if anyone <u>says</u> to this mountain, Go, throw yourself into the sea,' and does not doubt in his heart but believes that what he <u>says</u> will happen, it will be done for him. 24 Therefore I tell you, whatever you <u>ask</u> for in prayer, believe that you have received it, and it will be yours.

Ask, was used seven times in the verses above. Jesus wants us to speak!

What type of words should we be using when we pray? We should pray using God's promises and His Words of wisdom. God has Words to fit all of our situations. These are the words we should use when we pray. In other words we should be praying in agreement with God.

To be praying words of doubt, defeat, sickness, poverty, would not line up with God's words. They would line up with the devil. So it would put the devil in control of your prayer.

Many people pray... **"Oh God, I am so sick. I think I might die. Please heal me. (And then because they fear that He might not and have no idea what He is going to do, they add, if it be your will.)** Well they have just sided with the devil. The devil is controlling their life and they are agreeing with him. They did not come to God in faith. They just came hoping. They did not even take the time to find out what God's will was.

Their prayer should have been. **"The power of God is in me to put me over." "Greater is He that is in me than he that is in the world" "I'm quickened according to the word of God. I thank God that the ability of God is released in me. I stand before demons, I stand before sickness and disease, and I have no fear, because the Power and Authority of God is released within me, by the words of my mouth and by THE WORDS OF GOD. "Praise the name of the Lord." Dear Father, I am claiming what is mine. 1 Peter 2:24, By His Strips I am Healed!! Thank YOU Jesus.**

IN EVERY SITUATION IN LIFE, YOU NEVER LOSE, WHEN YOU TAKE SIDES WITH GOD!   LET GOD'S CREATIVE POWER WORK FOR YOU!

Jesus said, Matt 12:37 For by <u>your words</u> you will be acquitted, and by <u>your words</u> you will be condemned."

THE TREASURES OF YOUR HEART CANNOT BE HIDDEN. YOU ARE SPEAKING THEM CONSTANTLY. FOR VICTORY, MAKE SURE THAT THEY ARE THE WORDS OF GOD!

Watch your confessions:

Out of the abundance of the heart, the mouth speaks. So keep positive confessions in your heart. Do not let your mouth nullify your prayers. You cannot get results if you are letting your mouth side with the devil!

James 3:3-5 says, Your mouth needs to be bridled. It is like a rudder.... It can change your whole life. So start turning your life around...

Stop saying how bad you feel! Start speaking victory with the word of God.

"I am a conqueror!" *(Romans 8:37)* **"I can do all things through Christ who strengthens me!"** *(Philippians 4:13)* I don't have to bow down to the Devil again. **I have been redeemed from the curse of the law. (Gal 3:13)** I'm a child of the King.......I'll live like a King....I'll look like a King.... And I'll act like a King. Praise God, my needs are met... Praise God, I am healed... Praise God I have divine health... **(1 John 4:4) I am quickened according to the word of God.** The power of God is released in me by the words of my mouth and by the Word of God! Thank you Jesus!

Rom 8:11 And if the Spirit of him who raised Jesus from the dead is living in you, he who raised Christ from the dead will also give life to your mortal bodies through his Spirit, who lives in you. Are you reading that? Do you understand that? The same Spirit that was in Jesus is living in you. It makes mortal bodies alive! Spirit Words spoken by Jesus, ignites the faith that is residing in you! It causes an explosion of God's ability on your behalf when you speak these Spirit filled Words! Here is really what is happening...

Luke 17:6 Jesus said, "If you have faith as small as a mustard seed, you can say to this mulberry tree, 'Be uprooted and planted in the sea,' and it will obey you.

A mustard seed has a husk... Inside there is a tiny seed... When planted that seed burst forth and makes a mighty tree... You have a body, a husk... Inside you have a measure of faith, which God gave you. (Romans 12:3) That faith is held in your spirit which is joined with the Holy Spirit. (1 Cor. 6:17)

How do we activate this? Jesus says, when <u>We Speak</u> these forces come together and you have an explosion of God's Power working for you. Add the name of Jesus to this mix and every knee will bow. **Phil 2:10, that at the name of Jesus every knee should bow, in heaven and on earth and under the earth**, that is every evil spirit, every disease, everything in this universe. Praise God! And Jesus has given His name to us with the authority that goes with it. (Mark 16:17)(Luke 10:19)

What should we be doing with this Power?

John 14:12-14 I tell you the truth, anyone who has faith in me will do what I have been doing. He will do even greater things than these, because I am

going to the Father. 13 And I will do whatever you ask in my name, so that the Son may bring glory to the Father. 14 You may ask me for anything in my name, and I will do it.

Does that give you any idea how much Jesus loves you! We are followers of Christ. The Greek word for followers is "to imitate." So to use the power of the tongue perfectly we should follow or imitate how Jesus spoke.

1) When Jesus prayed, He always prayed what God said the answer was.
2) His conversation, always lined up with the word of God.
3) He never confessed the circumstances, always the end results.
4) He used the written word to defeat Satan. Like it is written, look in Mathew 4:4, 4:7, 4:10. You can too. **Tell Satan that you do not have cancer for it is written by His strips I am healed. Quote the verse 1 Peter 2:24, let the Devil know that you know what you posses.**
5) Jesus, always spoke directly to the problem, Winds, Trees, Storms. Satan and demons all had to obey Him. Not as the Son of God, but as the Son of man. Because, Jesus, came here as a human, He was laying the ground work for us showing us that we could use this power. Jesus was operating under the power of the Father's Word. You can do the same.

Say Aloud....
The God kind of faith believes in the heart, that what it says with the mouth will come to pass. And then dares to say it! Hallelujah!!!!!!

-----------------La Vern----------------

Cancers have been destroyed. Old diseased hearts made new. All of these were done inside the body. I knew they were real, but I did not get to see it happen. Well, one night while we were having a revival at my Church, a girl of about 22, with one leg 3" shorter than the other made her way down to the healing line. You can just imagine her coming down the isle, in the erratic walk. We sat her in a straight back chair and placed her feet out in another. You could plainly see how short the leg was. The church started praying. I, my Pastor, and a guest Pastor were right beside the girl. We held our hands over her, but did not touch her. I was at her feet, and could see her perfectly. We spoke the words of God over her body. As we prayed the leg got longer. We kept praying and praising. And in about four minutes the leg was the same length as the other. I watched it move out inch at a time. **Praise God... The word of "God works when we dare to say it!**

Faith is governed by the pure Word of God.....
And is nothing less than expecting God to do what He promises. We hope for what may be possible. But we have faith in and expect what God promises.
Because God Does Not Lie!

Chapter 8

Advanced: PROBLEM HEALING

Road blocks the Devil has set up, to rob you of God's gifts.

Some people have asked God for healing and nothing has happened... They think, God does not hear me...I am not worthy... Healing is only for a few... It must not be His will to heal me... **WHEN I PRAY NOTHING HAPPENS!**

You are not alone. Many people pray and do not get healed. WHY????

We are going to go over some of the most common causes for not being healed. See if you are in one of these groups. If so, **GET THE PROBLEM OUT and GET HEALED. God meant for you to have all of His blessings.**

1) Are you living the life God meant for you to live?
Third John 2, "Beloved, I wish above all things that you may prosper and be in health, even as your soul prospers." Here is what God wants for you. And one of the clues as to how we get it. Our prosperity and our health prosper as our soul prospers... Are we feeding our souls? Are we staying in the Word?

Or...are we letting our minds spend more time in the world with unbelievers?

II Cor.6:16b-18, God said, "I will live with them and walk among them, and I will be their God, and they will be my people." Therefore come out from them (the people of the world) and be separate. Touch no unclean thing, and I will receive you. I will be a Father to you, and you will be my sons and daughters."

Three things are important here. a) We can only be cleansed by the Blood of Jesus. b) Are we spending too much time with the wrong people? Letting their ways rub off onto us. c) We can be sons and daughters... And what do they get? **All of God's blessings, His love, His grace, His protection, His authority, His power. Sons of God may speak and it is done. They may bind things that are loose and loose things that are bound. Praise God!!**

**You cannot soar with Eagles,
And hang around with Buzzards!**

2) What do you want most, Healing or Jesus?

Psalm 37:4 Delight yourself in the Lord and He will give you the desires of your heart. Divine healing can only come to a Christian as a by product of loving Jesus. It is one of your gifts. Like Salvation and Eternal life. Test yourself and see. Do you want your healing the most? Or do you want to have a loving relationship with Jesus the most?

People come 2jesus all the time, about 3500 per day. Many come to be healed. Some just want to pull in like a filling station and say heal me and then go on their way. Living life the way they were living it before. Not searching for God, not wanting to follow in the way of Jesus. Just patch me up and send me out again. **Matt. 6:33 But seek first (First!! Not after you are healed but first.) His Kingdom and Righteousness, and all these things will be given to you as well. (What things?) All of God's promises.**

3) Come Expecting

----------------Indian Lady----------------

A lady from India came on the site. She said she had a skin disease. Many doctors had looked at it and no one even knew what it was or could cure it. She got red splotches on her face and then they would then raise up and turn crusty and black. Her face was now covered and she wore a hood over her head because she was so ugly to look at. We went over Jesus' teaching and then we prayed. In two week she wrote me back and said her face was as smooth and clear as a baby's. She said, "Now, please tell me about, Jesus." She probably was not a Christian before. But that was not for me to say. She had come to Jesus expecting..... And Jesus did not disappoint her. I prayed and Jesus healed her.... Now she is a Christian and a light to her family in India.

To come expecting, quickly gets Jesus attention. Look at these verses and see how Jesus operates.

Healing of a paralyzed man

Mark 2:1-5

1   A few days later, when Jesus again entered Capernaum, the people heard that he had come home.

2   So many gathered that there was no room left, not even outside the door, and he preached the word to them.

3   Some men came, bringing to him a paralytic, carried by four of them.

4   Since they could not get him to Jesus because of the crowd, they made an opening in the roof above Jesus and, after digging through it, lowered the mat the paralyzed man was lying on.

5   When Jesus saw their faith, he said to the paralytic, "Son, your sins are forgiven."

6   Now some teachers of the law were sitting there, thinking to themselves,

7   "Why does this fellow talk like that? He's blaspheming! Who can forgive sins but God alone?"

8   Immediately Jesus knew in his spirit that this was what they were thinking in their hearts, and he said to them, "Why are you thinking these things?

9   <u>Which is easier: to say to the paralytic, 'Your sins are forgiven,' or to say, 'Get up, take your mat and walk'?</u> (We under Jesus have the ability to have our sins forgiven anytime we feel the need)

10 But that you may know that the Son of Man has authority on earth to forgive sins...." He said to the paralytic,

11 "I tell you, get up, take your mat and go home."

12 He got up, took his mat and walked out in full view of them all. This amazed everyone and

they praised God, saying, "We have never seen anything like this!"

What did these men do? They came expecting. They came in faith, and they let nothing hold them back. They cut a hole in the roof to let the man down in front of Jesus. These men were expecting to have their friend healed.

Jairus came to get Jesus to heal his daughter.

Notice, Jairus, came to Jesus. His daughter was at home. His home was somewhere across town as he had to go there. Jairus, took action. He expected.

Mark 5:21-42
21 When Jesus had again crossed over by boat to the other side of the lake, a large crowd gathered around him while he was by the lake.
22 Then one of <u>the synagogue rulers, named Jairus, came there</u>. Seeing Jesus, he <u>fell at his feet</u> <u>(He humbled himself.)</u>
23 <u>and pleaded earnestly with him,</u> "My little daughter is dying. Please come and put your hands on her so that she will be healed and live."
24 <u>So Jesus went with him.</u> <u>(If you humbles yourself and prayed earnestly He would come with you too. With Jesus with you, something is going to happen.)</u> **A large crowd followed and pressed around him.**
25 And a woman was there who had been subject to bleeding for twelve years.

26 She had suffered a great deal under the care of many doctors and had spent all she had, yet instead of getting better she grew worse.

27 <u>When she heard about Jesus, she came </u>up behind him in the crowd and <u>touched his cloak,</u> <u>(Again she took action, she was expecting.)</u>

28 because she thought, "If I just touch his clothes, I will be healed."

29 Immediately her bleeding stopped and she felt in her body that she was freed from her suffering.

She pushed through the crowd. This woman had stopped Jesus from where He was going. She came expecting, believing, in faith. She did not let anyone or anything hold her back.

30 <u>At once Jesus realized that power had gone out from him.</u> <u>(Jesus knows when you touch Him.</u> <u>When you come in faith.)</u> He turned around in the crowd and asked, "Who touched my clothes?"

31 "You see the people crowding against you," his disciples answered, "and yet you can ask, 'Who touched me?'"

32 But Jesus kept looking around to see who had done it.

33 Then the woman, knowing what had happened to her, came and fell at his feet and, trembling with fear, told him the whole truth.

34 He said to her, "Daughter, your faith has healed you. Go in peace and be freed from your suffering."

35 While Jesus was still speaking, some men came from the house of Jairus, the synagogue ruler.

"Your daughter is dead," they said. "Why bother the teacher any more?"

36 Ignoring what they said, Jesus told the synagogue ruler, "Don't be afraid; just believe." (Bad news did not waver Jesus faith. Do not let bad news waver yours.)

37 He did not let anyone follow him except Peter, James and John the brother of James. (Why? He did not want unbelievers around. You do not either.)

38 When they came to the home of the synagogue ruler, Jesus saw a commotion, with people crying and wailing loudly.

39 He went in and said to them, "Why all this commotion and wailing? The child is not dead but asleep."

40 But they laughed at him. (Again He cast out the unbelievers)

After he put them all out, he took the child's father and mother and the disciples who were with him, and went in where the child was.

41 He took her by the hand and said to her, "Talitha koum!" (which means, "Little girl, I say to you, get up!").

42 Immediately the girl stood up and walked around (she was twelve years old). At this they were completely astonished.

The Pastor that ordained me said that Jesus was speaking in tongues here. That the writers did not know what He said, but put in, "Little girl, I say to you get up." Because that is what happened.

What did the father do? He went and found Jesus. He came Expecting and in Faith. He did not let the unbelief of others destroy his faith, he believed in Jesus.

Blind man on the street

Mark 10:46-52
46 Then they came to Jericho. As Jesus and his disciples, together with a large crowd, were leaving was the city, a blind man, Bartimaeus (that is, the Son of Timaeus), was sitting by the roadside begging.
47 <u>When he heard that it was Jesus of Nazareth, he began to shout</u>, "Jesus, Son of David, have mercy on me!" <u>(Make sure you are telling people about Jesus. So they will have heard. If he had not heard of Jesus he would not have called.)</u>
48 Many rebuked him and told him to be quiet, but he shouted all the more, "Son of David, have mercy on me!" <u>(Jesus was stopped by faith.)</u>
49 Jesus stopped and said, "Call him." So they called to the blind man, "Cheer up! On your feet! He's calling you."
50 Throwing his cloak aside, he jumped to his feet and came to Jesus.
51 "What do you want me to do for you?" Jesus asked him. The blind man said, "Rabbi, I want to see."
52 "Go," said Jesus, "your faith has healed you." Immediately he received his sight and followed Jesus along the road.

What had happened, the same as the others. He cried out with, Expectation. Many rebuked him and told him to be quite. He would not stop calling. He had faith and Jesus was stopped by his faith.

My first healing:

The Doctors said that I would die shortly or if I lived, be an invalid the rest of my life. I heard a voice say, "Jesus is the answer." This voice could have been just in my head, I do not know, it sounded real. You see I knew nothing really about how to access the Power of God. So Jesus, had to kick start me.

Do you think the woman with the issue of blood heard the same voice? The blind and the lame did they hear the voice? Have you ever heard the voice? Maybe I could be that voice for you, **"Jesus is the answer."**

That was all I needed to give me hope. With hope came a measure of faith, so I went and got my wife and my son and we came, Expecting. I did not know how to pray. But I knew what I wanted. So I said the world's simplest pray. "Dear Jesus, please heal me."

There was a snap in my chest and I knew that I was healed. That was in 1988. Thank you Jesus. Do not be bashful step out. When an alter call is made, be first in line. Be eager, Expect Jesus to do just what He said that He would.

Come Expecting…. Come Believing… Come in Faith…
Do not let anyone or anything hold you back.

4) You say, "God does not hear me, or it may not be God's will to heal me."

Isaiah 30:19, (How gracious He will be when you cry for help. As soon as He hears, He will answer you.) As soon as He hears? How do we know He hears? **Isaiah 65:24, (Before they call I will answer; while they are still speaking I will hear.) Job 22:27, (You will pray to Him and He will hear you.) 1 John 5:14-15, (This is the assurance we have in approaching God: that if we ask anything according to His will, He hears us. And if we know He hears us-whatever we ask- we know we have what we ask of Him.)**

Plus many more verses…

Now we know He hears us. But are you asking according to His will???? As we are talking about healing, yes, we know that is His will. All the way through the Bible God's will is for us to be healed. **James 5:14-16, Matt. 9:28-30, Matt. 9: 6-7, Matt. 4:23-24, Jeremiah 30:17, Exodus 23:25, 1 Peter 2:24, Isaiah 53:5… 3rd John 1-2** These are a few verses that prove that it is God's will to heal you.

IF THERE IS ANY DOUBT, LOOK AT JESUS… JESUS IS GOD'S WILL IN ACTION. AND HEALING WAS A CENTRAL PART OF HIS MINISTRY. JESUS NEVER TURNED ANYONE AWAY. ALL THEY HAD TO DO WAS BELIEVE AND ACT ON THAT BELIEF.

Look at these verses: Matt. 15:31, Luke 4:40, Luke 6:17 These verses shows that it is God's will to heal all who come in faith.

You can gauge anything on Jesus' life. Like some people believe God made them sick for punishment... Did you ever see Jesus make anyone sick? NO! Well God does not either.

If this was your problem, put your mind at rest. **God hears you and He wants you well.** Because, if you doubt God, you will get nothing. It would mean you did not have faith in His Word.

5) Are you walking in Love?

If we are to live in line with God's Word we must have love along with our faith. Are you walking in love? Read **1st Corinthians 13:1-13** This chapter is about love and how important God thinks it is. **Without love we are not Christ like.** Without love we are just going through the motions of faith and believing in Christ. Without love we cannot have the gifts God has in store for us.

Are you unknowingly not walking in love? If you find fault with someone do you rush to the phone to tell someone else what you found out? Or do you cover that fault with love and silence and try to restore that person. Quietly come to that person and go to the Lord in prayer.

If you gloat over other's mistakes, and in the next breath pray to God to heal you... your faith cannot work at the highest level. It probably will not work at all.

Do you hold grudges? If someone has wronged you, do you forgive them? You must forgive them!!!! Do not carry that burden of hate in your heart!!! You should forgive as God forgave you, with love. You should pray for them. You must pray, Lord, bless them. Lord, help them. They do not know what they are doing. Help them because they do not understand.

You say that is hard you cannot do that... Well tell me, has anyone pushed a crown of thorns down on your head? Has anyone whipped your back until it was cut to the bone and bleeding? Has anyone nailed your hands and feet to a cross and hung you up to die? Well they did that to our Jesus and He said, **"Forgive them for they do not know what they do."** If my Jesus can do that, then I have enough of his love in me to forgive someone who says something to hurt my feelings, or spreads untruths about me. And you do too.

Until we can do that, it will be hard to get well. The Devil will be in control of your life and not Jesus. Look back at <u>Mark 11:25 And when you stand praying, if you hold anything against anyone, forgive him, so that your Father in heaven may forgive you your sins."</u>

So as of this minute get the love of Christ into your life and GET HEALED!

6) I am not worthy.
Well maybe you are not. Let's see what that means. Is it because God does not think you are worthy, <u>Or because you do not feel worthy?</u>

If God thinks you are unworthy it will be for one reason only, you are living in sin. That is a sin you have not confessed to Him. Once you have confessed that sin to God, you will be immediately forgiven and be back in grace. And God will think of these sins no more. **Hebrews 8:12** And neither should you.

Look what Jesus has done for you. **1 John 2:1-2 If anyone sins we have one who speaks to the Father in our defense... Jesus Christ, the Righteous One. He is the atoning sacrifice for our sins and not only for ours but for the sins of the whole world... Thank you Jesus!**

So if you are not in sin and you still feel unworthy? Why? Who are you anyway?

How does God see you? Who are you in Christ?

Eph. 2:6, God has raised us up together with Christ.

In God's eyes you are seated with Jesus at His right hand. You are in Christ, just as Christ is in you here on earth. <u>You are worthy to be seated at the right hand of God.</u>

1Cor. 6:17, He that is joined to the Lord is one spirit.

You and Jesus could be no closer together. Jesus is not just with you, you are part of each other. Jesus the Son of God lives within you... <u>You are worthy...</u>

1Cor. 12:27, Now, you are the body of Christ.

He is the Head... You are the body... The head does the thinking and the leading, and the body carries out the work. So when Jesus wants something done here on earth it is up to you to do it. You and Jesus are working together hand and hand. <u>You are a worthy partner of, Jesus.</u>

Eph. 3:20, His power is at work in us.

His power is not dormant! It is at work. That means we are, or should be using it. <u>Jesus would not give His power to an unworthy person.</u>

John 17:22, Jesus said, "I have given them the Glory that you gave me..."

Jesus has given us... That is you and me... The glory that God had given Him... <u>Do you fully realize what a gift that is? You are exalted as Jesus is... You are a child of God. A brother or sister of Jesus, with all of the benefits... What God has is yours.</u>

John 17:23, Jesus said, "God has loved them, even as he had loved me."

Jesus is telling you that God loves you in the same way that He loves Jesus. What greater honor could be yours?

Matt. 28:20, Jesus said, "And I am always with you."

Jesus is always with us...always.... <u>Would He be with you if you were unworthy?</u>

2 Cor. 6:16, For we are the temple of the living God!

We are the temple.... Your body, That's where God is residing... He is not in the Church building, not unless you are there... <u>Because He is in you!</u>

NOW, THAT IS WORTHY?

If you still feel unworthy, that will be a lie the Devil is trying to get you to doubt God's love. And that is easily taken care of..... Jesus has given you control over the Devil, and the power to use His name. **Mark 16:17 and Luke 10:19**. All you have to do is use what Jesus has given you. **And that is the Name that All Heaven and Earth will bow too... Thank you Jesus!!**

You Command the Devil! Here is what you say... **Devil, you foul creature... I command you in the name of Jesus to take this spirit of unworthiness out of me. I belong to Jesus and it is written in Mark 16:17 & Luke 10:19... That I have control over you... So loose this sprit and command it to leave in the name of Jesus! I am worthy... I am a Child of God!**

You can use that power for any sneaky thing the Devil or any of his demons try to burden you down with. This is also the first thing I use on any sickness. As almost all illnesses are from the Devil. If that was your problem don't wait!

Get right with God! And get the Devil out of your life! And GET HEALED!

7) I Prayed for My Healing; But it does not seem Real.

Have you ever acted as if it were real? Have you ever told anyone that it is real?

Have you ever confessed it to be so? **Why, because you do not want to sound like a fool? Why? The Bible says it is so... Is the Bible a lie?** Are you afraid to walk out on faith... Are afraid to put God to the test... You say, "What if I don't get healed? I do not want to loose my faith in God." You want to give God an out just in case He does not want to heal you? Which all means you do not really believe, He is going to do it... Where is your faith?

Hebrews 4:2 But the message that they heard was of no value to them, because those who heard did not combine it with faith... This is a promise from God... If He, did not want you to have it, God, would not have given it to you!

You trust God with your future in eternity... Certainly you can trust Him with your health.... Because trusting for Salvation takes more faith then trusting Him for your healing.... **God's Word means what it says. STAND ON IT.**

Romans 10:10, with the mouth confession is made unto... A promise from God's Word must be confessed as a reality before it become true in your life...

Confess it... Claim it... Walk in it...
You are taking what is legally yours.

Say out loud......
God's word means what it says...
God is able to fulfill any promise He has made...
I believe God is talking to me, because I am a child of God...
Because I am a child of God... all His blessings are mine...
I have been healed by the strips of Jesus...
Therefore I claim this promise... Jesus it is mine!!!! I am well...

Praise God... Thank you Jesus... Hallelujah... Glory... Glory...

7) Worry... It can kill you!

Do you worry about your healing? Worry is unbelief... If you believed, you would not worry... With worry comes fear... And with fear faith leaves, and when faith leaves God has no way to contact you... You are all alone.

What does God say about worry?

(Philippians 4:6-7) 6) Do not be anxious about anything, but in everything, by prayer and petition, with thanksgiving, present your request to God. 7) And the peace of God, which transcends all understanding, will guard your hearts and your minds in Christ Jesus.

That is a command from God. **Do not be anxious about anything, but in everything, by prayer and petition, with thanksgiving, present your request to God.** You not only do not have to worry, He is telling you not too. He is telling you that if you have something to worry about to give it to Him, through prayer and petition, with thanksgiving. If you are thanking Him that means He has already taken care of it, or will shortly. If you have prayed for your healing, you must realize that it is in God's hands now... And God will not let you down... We must learn to trust Gods word. And what kind of peace is He going to give you? **And the peace of God, which transcends all understanding, will guard your hearts and your minds in Christ Jesus.** I can tell you that is total, beyond your imagination peace.

(1 Peter 5:7) Cast all your anxiety on Him because He cares for you.

Again, not some of your cares, all of them. Why, **because He cares for you.** If you love your children wouldn't you do that for them? Of course you would. Well we can't begin to comprehend the love God has for us. He sent His only Son to sacrifice Himself for us so we could live with Him forever. All He wants is your love and faith in Jesus. Trust Him, take Him at His word. Try it and watch your worries leave. After all think on this.

(Matthew 6:27) Who of you by worrying can add a single hour to his life?

On the contrary you will take years off of your life.

Say this aloud.... Psalm # 91:14-16
14. "Because he loves Me," says the Lord, "I will rescue him; I will protect him, <u>for he acknowledges my name.</u>
15. He will call upon Me, and I will answer him; I will be with him in trouble, I will deliver him and honor him.
16. With long life will I satisfy him and show him my salvation."

8) DO NOT EVER BE ASHAMED OF JESUS!!!

Matt. 10:32-33, Jesus said, "Whoever acknowledges me before men, I will also acknowledge him before my Father in Heaven... But whoever disowns me before men, I will disown him before my Father in Heaven."

Jesus said this to me on 10/12/99, I was having a problem, a large one. So I ask God for help. Jesus spoke these words to me.

He said, "I will protect you...   I will fight your battle...

He that is in you is greater than the world...

I will lift you up in my Father's house,

And say, this one is mine..."

Thank you my Savior... I am telling you this for two reasons. One, if the Lord ever speaks to you it will always line up with scripture... If it does not line up, it could be the Devil, trying to trick you. Second, The Lord is watching you... Whether He speaks or not... He is with you and He knows exactly what you are going through... He is there for you... Do not be shy!!! Call His name... Humble yourself and ask for help... It is His pleasure to be there for His children. He has given you many promises... Claim them...

9) The Big One...Weak Faith

This is a killer... You will surly die of some disease if you do not have faith. You have just read what you have in Christ and where you are positioned in God's eyes. So that should be a big start in letting you know what can be done through faith and that God means for you to have faith and to use the power and gifts He has given you. Why would He have given them to you, if He did not want you to use them? Besides it is our duty to be the Body of Christ here on earth, and doing His work for Him as He directs. **You cannot do that without all the tools He has given you. Faith is your #1 tool.**

(Hebrews 4:2 But the message that they heard was of no value to them, because those who heard did not combine it with faith.)

People build faith by listening to God's Word and reading (aloud) God's Word.

Romans 10:17 Faith comes by hearing and hearing by the Word of God.

So start building faith. Do you listen to more TV than you listen to God's word? That may let you know why you are not healed.

Do you trust God's Word above everything else? If God says you are healed, do you believe it? Or do you believe the doctor or your body's pain?

Here is how faith works. You pray for your healing. And now comes the hard part... When you believe in your heart that you have been healed, <u>you are healed!</u> No matter what your body says. You believe it because that is what God's word says. At that moment you accept your healing from the Spirit world. And it is yours... Also at that moment you start praising God and thanking Him for the healing He has given you.... And then God, through your faith in Him, and the power of the Holy Spirit, brings it into the natural and you are then healed physically. I hope you got that because it is how God operates and the most important thing you will ever know about divine healing.

Think about it this way. And this is the way most people think about it. If you pray and then wait for the healing to manifest in the physical before you start thanking God. That does not take faith... Any atheist could do that.

Now how long do you wait for your healing to manifest into the natural world? That is a good question with no real accurate answer. I have been healed many times. Two of my healing were instant. One took about two weeks and another took about a year, although I was feeling better right after I prayed and then I got better and better everyday for the next year and then it was completely gone. I have been connected with many other people who have been healed and their headings were the same. Some instant, some, over a period of time.

Now here is how a lot of people loose their healing. They start off fine. They have the faith it takes and they are healed. But they do not see it in the natural and after a while with the Devil shouting at them that it is not going to work..... That God did not hear them pray, or they were unworthy, or some other lie, they give up on God. And at that time they lost their healing that was working in their body. So when our healing is not instant, how are we to keep the Devil at bay while we wait?

1st. Timothy 6:12, We are to fight the good fight of faith. We have to believe God and trust in His word. We are going to have to hold our ground... Even when it looks like we are going down... **But do not quit! Through God you will be victorious... Just believe His word and do not give up.**

Get into the Word and build your faith. Then go back out and meet the Devil head on and say,

"There is nothing you can do to me..." **Jesus has given me the power to defeat you and the one who is in me is greater than anything this world can throw at me.** If you are going to beat the Devil in every situation in life, **you must have an attitude that you refuse to quit!**

Your timetable is not the same as God's. We are impatient. We want now! Well God may have a different idea. Remember, He can give you a miracle, but He does not promise that. He promises you healing. Many times that may take several months. But remember you were healed the moment you prayed and you claimed it.

I look at it this way. When I pray, I receive God's healing power into my spirit. It is mine, I have it... I am healed... From that time on I praise God and thank Him for my healing. If a pain or symptom comes to me I say, "in the name of Jesus, you must leave, Jesus has healed me and you can no longer stay in my body."

1 Tim. 6:12, I will fight the good fight of faith.

So do not give in to impatience. Do not give up and say "Well I guess it was not for me."   Here is how God instructs you on how to act.

Hebrews 10:35-36 So do not throw away your confidence; it will be richly rewarded. You need to persevere so that when you have done the will of God, you will receive what He has promised.

What you have just read is so important. You must learn how to accept your gift.

Chapter 9

Summery of Divine Healing
James 5:14-15 The prayer of faith will save the sick..

WHAT IS THE PRAYER OF FAITH?

Jesus tells us what it is and how to use it.

Mark 11:24 Therefore I tell you, <u>whatever you ask for in prayer, believe that you have received it, and it will be yours.</u>

There were two stipulations here.
1) **You must ask for it.**
   Not think about it.... Or write a letter... you must ask!
   Romans 10:8, The word is near you; it is in your mouth and in your   heart, that is the word of faith we are proclaiming.
2) **Believe that you have received it..**
   Not going to believe it... No! Believe it now... When you pray is NOW!
   You see God only deals in the now... God says, "I AM" which is now.
   Not I was or I will be. **(Here people really get in trouble. They say, "I hope I   will be healed or I know that someday God will heal me.")**
   <u>These people will receive nothing from God.. Because God only deals in faith.</u>

When you have a gun, you have a triggering devise to release the power. You also have a triggering device to release the Power of God. <u>It is faith!</u>

Jesus said, "whatever you ask for in prayer, <u>believe that you have received it,</u> and it will be yours."

So how do you believe something that you do not have?

With faith.. **Hebrew 11:1 For faith is the substance of things hoped for the evidence of things not seen.**

So you must believe in God's word. God's word becomes the evidence of things hoped for. You can grab hold of your Bible and say this is the substance of my healing or whatever you prayed for. It is the same as a contract. Only this one is with God. **And it is impossible for God to lie. Hebrew 6:18**

So FAITH is the triggering device to release the power of God.

Mark 11:24, and it will be yours. That is when your prayer will be manifested to you in this physical world. That might be a few minutes or days or even months. But it was yours the moment you prayed. So at that moment you should start thanking God.

What if you prayed this same prayer again? Many of us pray the same prayer over and over. Do you think God is deaf? Each time you do this you cancel out the first prayer and start waiting all over again. It would mean that you did not believe that you had received. If that was what you believed then that is what you will get. Nothing!

So what do you do while you are waiting? You praise God and thank Him. And you can say that the Power of God is working mightily in me, bringing the gift that I have received into the natural. Thank you Jesus!!!!

Mark 11:24 What ever you desire... That sounds like anything. It is. It is anything that God has promised to give you. Which covers everything that you will need here in this life that is good and is not evil? He has even given you a catalog of all the wonderful things to choose from. The Bible!

So when you are praying for a particular blessing from God, you could think of it as ordering from a **"Spiritual Mail Order Company."** We order things every day. And we take it on faith that the company will deliver. We trust man. Why can't we trust God?

The Bible is your catalog. Check to see if your blessing is covered and note the verse. You will use this in your prayer to let God know that this is what you are claiming.

Now we order it from the Spirit world by prayer. (the company) We give God our order. Specified the verse... (the catalog number) Tell God that we came in the name of Jesus and that He has paid our bill. (Gave the company our credit card.) Now all we have to do is wait for delivery... But it was ours just as soon as we were charged for it and the credit card was cleared.

So when do we get delivery? In the natural it could go regular mail, air mail, express mail. It depends on what we paid for. Spiritually, it is the same, except we pay by faith. The speed will be in direct proportion to your faith.

Jesus told the Centurion, Matt. 8:13, "Go your way and as you believed, (or as of your faith) so let it be done for you." And his servant was healed that same hour.

But are you a doubting Thomas? Are you asking, "Well how do I know that God heard my prayer?" *1 John 5:14-15, This is the confidence that we have in approaching God: that if we ask anything according to His will He hears us. And if we know He hears us - whatever we ask - we know that we have what we ask of Him.*

You say well how do I know if it is God's will? You read the Bible. God tells you what His will is. If in doubt... Look at Jesus... Jesus was God's will in action.

Now listen to Jesus as He tells us how to get all the blessing out of this life. *How to live as Kings here on earth.*

John 20:24-29 Now, Thomas, one of the twelve, was not with the disciples when Jesus came. So the other disciples told him, "We have seen the Lord!" But Thomas said to them, "Unless I see the marks in His hands and put my fingers where the nails were, and put my hand into His side, I will not believe it."

A week later His disciples were in the house again and Thomas was with them. Though the doors were locked, Jesus came and stood among them and said, "Peace be with you!" Then He said to Thomas, "Put your finger here; see my hands. Reach out your hand and put it into my side. Stop *doubting and believe." Thomas said to Him, "My Lord and my God!" then Jesus told him, "Because you have seen me, you have believed; <u>blessed are those who have not seen and yet have believed.</u>"*

Are you a doubting Thomas???? Are you one of the Blessed????

If blessed say, "Praise God! Thank you Jesus!"

"Praise God! Thank you Jesus!"

<u>AND RECEIVE!</u>

But if you still are having problems believing, is there any hope left for you? Yes, Jesus shows us in Mark 9:23-27

Mark 9:23-27

23 Jesus said unto him, If thou can believe, all things are possible to him that believes.

24 And straightway the father of the child cried out, and said with tears, Lord, I believe; help thou mine unbelief.

25 When Jesus saw that the people came running together, he rebuked the foul spirit, saying unto him, Thou dumb and deaf spirit, I charge thee, come out of him, and enter no more into him.

26 And the spirit cried, and rent him sore, and came out of him: and he was as one dead; insomuch that many said, He is dead.

27 But Jesus took him by the hand, and lifted him up; and he arose.

You see if you humble yourself and ask for help, Jesus, will join His faith to yours. As you saw the boy was healed and the father had doubts. We will never fully conceive how great Jesus' love is for us. **Thank you Jesus.**

Ps 86:5 For thou, Lord, art good, and ready to forgive; and plenteous in mercy unto all them that call upon thee.

Sayings to keep your mind in line
The word of God works. When you do what it says. I am fully persuaded that what God's word says, He is able to do!
> *So if He says I have it, I have it.*
> *If He says I will receive it, I will receive it!*
> **God can not and will not lie!!!!!**
> **Hebrews 6:18**

The God kind of faith believes in the heart, that what it says with the mouth will come to pass. And then dares to say it!

Psalm 18:21
> **Jesus, has the power to perform what He has promised you.**
> **Jesus, will do what He has promised you...**
> **All you have to do is accept what Jesus has promised you. Praise God! Romans 4:21**
> **Thank You Jesus!**

Faith is governed by the pure Word of God.....And is nothing less than expecting God to do what He promises.

We hope for what may be possible.

But we have faith in and expect what God promises.

Because God Does Not Lie!

**DO NOT LET THE DEVIL TAKE AWAY YOUR FAITH!
YOU ARE HEALED AND GOD WILL BRING IT FORTH!**

Matt. 18:19, Jesus says, "Again, I tell you that if two of you on earth agree about anything you ask for, it will be done for you by my Father in Heaven, for where two or three come together in my name, there am I with them.

So we know that Jesus is with us... And Jesus has promised that if we agree the prayer will be answered... Ferd and I will stand in agreement. Let us pray...

DEAR FATHER I STAND IN AGREEMENT ON (MATT.18:19) WITH FERD. WE KNOW I AM HEALED BECAUSE YOUR WORD SAYS THAT I AM AND I BELIEVE AND TRUST IN YOUR WORD. WE ARE STANDING ON YOUR PROMISES AND WE KNOW YOU CANNOT LIE. SO WE ARE ASSURED THAT I HAVE MY HEALING.

I NOW HAVE GOTTEN MY HEART IN THE RIGHT POSITION TO RECEIVE. I LOVE JESUS MORE THAN LIFE. I WANT TO FOLLOW JESUS AND HIS WAYS. I WANT TO SHOUT JESUS' PRAISES AND TELL THE WORLD OF HIS GREAT HEALING. FATHER WE ARE CONFESSING TO YOU AND TO THE WORLD THAT I AM HEALED.

AND I AM READY FATHER TO HAVE MY HEALING BROUGHT INTO THE NATURAL. WE STAND TOGETHER SAYING THAT THE DEVIL CANNOT KEEP IT AWAY FROM ME WITH LIES ANY LONGER. THANK YOU FATHER, YOUR LOVING CHILDREN, FERD AND I, WE PRAY IN THE PRECIOUS NAME OF OUR SAVIOR, JESUS... AMEN.

Now Father we will use the Power of Jesus, that He has given to us. Mark 16:17 and Luke 10:19. <u>Shout this to the walls where you are, or go out into the yard.</u>

BODY, BE HEALED IN JESUS NAME... SATAN YOU VILE CREATURE. WE TAKE AUTHORITY OVER YOU IN THE NAME OF JESUS, THE NAME ABOVE ALL NAMES. JESUS, HAS DEFEATED YOU AND IT IS WRITTEN THAT HE HAS GIVEN US, HIS AUTHORITY TO CAST YOU OUT OF OUR LIVES.... ANY DISEASE IN MY BODY HAS TO LEAVE NOW. BE LOOSED, SHRIVEL UP AND DIE YOU DEMON FROM HELL, YOU CAN NOT STAY IN MY BODY ANY LONGER. IN JESUS NAME, OUT OF MY BODY, OUT OF MY LIFE. THE ONE THAT IS IN ME, JESUS, IS GREATER THAN ANYTHING IN THIS WORLD AND YOU SATAN, HAVE NO POWER AGAINST JESUS.... I AM HEALED, MY HEALING WAS PAID FOR BY JESUS AND IT IS MINE.... I TAKE IT AND COMMAND YOU TO LEAVE, FOR I AM TAKING WHAT IS MINE! THANK YOU JESUS FOR DELIVERING ME, THANK YOU FOR MAKING ME WHOLE. THANK YOU FOR BEING IN MY LIFE. WE LOVE YOU AND SERVE YOU WITH ALL OF OUR HEART, MYSELF AND FERD, AMEN...

YOU NOW HAVE YOUR HEALING AND YOU ARE GOING TO FIGHT THE GOOD FIGHT OF FAITH AND THE DEVIL IS NOT GOING TO KEEP IT FROM YOU. YOU USE THIS COMMAND AND CONFESS YOUR HEALING AND PRAISE GOD EVERYDAY.........

WE ARE NOT GOING TO PUT UP WITH THE DEVIL ANY LONGER... HE IS DEFEATED, DEFEATED, DEFEATED, DEFEATED, DEFEATED, DEFEATED, **DEFEATED, DEFEATED, DEFEATED, DEFEATED!**

Chapter 10

HEALING IN A NUT SHELL!

1) **Say it**. Confess that you are going to be healed by Jesus.
2) **Do it. Take action.** Look for the scriptures that promise your healing.
   Then search for God in prayer and faith.
3) **Use the power that Jesus has given you.** Cast out the sickness...
4) **Receive it.** Grab hold of your healing in faith and claim it. (Agree with God's Word.) (Not what your body says.)(Physical healing will follow.)
5) **Tell it**. Confess it, so others may believe.

Here is a perfect Word to say everyday to stay in good health.

Christ has redeemed me from the curse of the law. Therefore, I forbid any sickness or disease to come upon my body. Every germ and every virus that touches my body dies instantly in the name of Jesus. Every organ and every tissue of my body functions in the perfection to which God created it to function, and I forbid any malfunction in my body, in the name of Jesus. (Gal 3:13. Rom 8:11, Gen 1:30, Matt. 16:19.) I am healed for Jesus paid for my healing at the Cross, that it might be fulfilled which was spoken

by Isaiah the prophet, saying, Himself took my infirmities, and bare my sicknesses. For by His stripes I am healed. Jesus carried all of my diseases and infirmities. All I need to do is receive it and confess it.

Thank you Jesus. (I Peter 2:24, Matt. 8:17)

My Prayer for You!

I pray for everyone who reads this that their healing will be swift and complete. That the Lord Jesus will guide you into the perfect peace that He has for each of you. That your battles with the Devil will be small and victorious. I also pray that as you receive your healing you will go forth and sing the praises of Jesus. Let the world know that God's word is true and that through Him you are more than a conqueror... Much, much more...

In Christ, Ferd

Chapter 11

2 Jesus Praise Reports

I have put in a few of the Testimonies that I have gotten on 2Jesus.org. You can not get enough Testimonies as that is how you defeat the Devil.

Rev 12:11 And they overcame him (the Devil) by the blood of the Lamb, (Jesus) and by the word of their testimony;

I have put this Testimony first as you have just read the book about Jesus' healing power. Now I will show you this power working people's lives.

The Power of Jesus

From Africa, Evang. John Aakiel

Dear Brothers and Sisters in Christ, This is Ferd@2jesus, I want to give Jesus a praise report. Also I want to make sure that you know what you possess as a Christian. So many Christians go through life and never figure out what they possess. Isn't that a shame as Jesus paid such a price for us to get it.

I will tell you a story about a man in Africa. His name is John. He is an Evangelist. He is a man of God. He has saved many people. But never really realized who he was in Christ, what he really possessed. John came to 2jesus with a problem.

He had two children that he had taken in. They were very sick. They both needed an operation to live. John had taken them to the hospital. He gave them all the money that he had. He was still short $100. Without the extra $100, they would not operate. He came 2jesus for the money.

To send $100 to save two children seems a small price to pay. I probably should have sent it... However that is not what the Holy Spirit led me to send. I immediately sat down and wrote this letter.

Dear John,

Jesus, does not want these children to die... You have the ability to heal them through Christ. You are working for Christ with all of your heart. You have faith in Him. You know the power that is in Him. But do you believe that Jesus has given it to you? Look at these words from Jesus. Please read them and fill your spirit with them.

Mark 11:23-24
23 For verily I say unto you, That whosoever shall say unto this mountain, Be thou removed, and be thou cast into the sea; and shall not doubt in his heart, but shall believe that those things which he saith shall come to pass; he shall have whatsoever he saith.

24 Therefore I say unto you, What things soever ye desire, when ye pray, believe that ye receive them, and ye shall have them.

John, Jesus is talking to you. Have you ever thought who you are in Christ?

Eph. 2:6, God has raised us up together with Christ.

In God's eyes you are seated with Jesus at His right hand. You are in Christ, just as Christ is in you here on earth.

1Cor. 6:17, He that is joined to the Lord is one spirit.

You and Jesus could be no closer together. Jesus is not just with you, you are part of each other.

1Cor. 12:27, Now you are the body of Christ.

What does that mean? We Christians here on earth are the body of Christ. He is the Head. The head does the thinking and the leading, and the body carries out the work. So when Jesus wants something done here on earth it is up to us to do it. How could we? Easy, with Jesus' Spirit joined to ours He is transferring His authority and power to us to do His will. But we must except it and be obedient to His commands.

Matt. 28:20, "And I am always with you."

All power belongs to Jesus ... and Jesus is always with us. So we have that power in us at all times.

Eph. 3:20, His power is at work in us.

His power is not dormant! It is at work. That means we are, or should be using it. How many of us are really using it? Isn't it time we realized what Jesus has done for us and start doing what He intended. Being His body here on Earth and carrying out the Father's will.

HOW MUCH POWER IS THAT?

Matt. 28:18, Jesus said, "All power is given to me in Heaven and Earth."

Eph. 11:19-20, His power is like He used to raise Jesus. Hallelujah!!!

That is the power to raise the dead. That is the power to heal the sick. That is the power to trample the Devil and all evil forces that come against us. That is the power to be the Body of Christ.

THAT IS THE POWER OF GOD! ... THANK YOU JESUS... WHAT HAS GOD MADE YOU? 1 JOHN 3:1 HOW GREAT IS THE LOVE THE FATHER HAS LAVISHED ON US, THAT WE SHOULD BE CALLED CHILDREN OF GOD! AND THAT IS WHAT WE ARE!

But you can only use a gift that you know you have, and that you accept. And we can only use it through Jesus, because of God's grace and love for us.

IT TOOK ME 12 YR. OF STUDY BEFORE GOD REVELED TO ME WHO I WAS IN CHRIST.

John, when you can get those verses down in your spirit you will be able to use the power that Jesus has given you.

Go to that hospital and lay your hands on those children and say, "In the name of Jesus be healed." and do not doubt, start thanking God for their healing. By the time the doctor gets there he will be asking what happened to them ... Thank you Jesus...

I am not trying to tell you things to be smart, like I am wiser than you. No, you already know these things. But sometimes we get so busy in the natural that we forget (or the devil hides it from us) what Jesus has given us. We can not do all that He wants us to do without the tools that He has given us.

Give it a try. Go pray for these children. I will pray for you and the children on this end. Keep your faith strong. For as you go out to use the power that Jesus has given you the devil will try to steal it from you with doubt. For if he can do that he will have defeated you and you will not be able to stand against him. So always remember. I John 4:4 Ye are of God, little children, and have overcome them: because greater is he that is in you, than he that is in the world.

Your brother in Christ, Ferd

A week later I got this letter from John...

Dear Brother in Christ,

Greetings and salutation in the marvelous name of our heavenly father, and our Lord Jesus Christ, who suffered for our sins that He might bring us to God. And by Him to be saved. I give thanks to the father for His infinite love and grace He has toward us, may He bless and keep you from evil, may His face shine upon you and peace.

I thank God so much for His victory given us in Christ Jesus and for His healing power of His word that has broken every stronghold in our lives. My visit to the children was blessed; I examine the anointing power of His word as it was proclaimed. I prayed and fasted through the power of the Holy spirit and the Lord spoke to me so beautifully,

He said by His stripe ye have healed, I felt it with gratitude and I rose to the full power of my faith for healing, and I laid my hand on the children and prayed, I felt and believe it in my heart that the children is going to be heal, and I spoke forth His word and the healing came forth in their body and they where completely healed. <u>One of the children said that he saw a great man, holding His hand and said to him be healed my son, for I am the Lord thy God.</u>

After I heard this from the children, I began to give praises and honor, to His Holy name, the doctors where so surprise to see the manifestation of His healing power to the children, they were again tested by the doctors and it showed that they were alright, healed. From them, the word of God was confirmed; the doctor believed and embraces Jesus as the Lord of their life. After sharing Christ with them in the hospital, I promised to come back to them for a visit and come along with the word of God, the Bible, to share with them to build up their faith and knowing more of His perfect revelation to man kind, thanks be to God, the Healer of our refuge, He said His word, "lift up your eye from the battle to the victory, for Christ is already victor, although we do not see all things under His feet they are there, Heb., 2:8.

I thank you for your marvelous work in the Lord and of your given heart. What a great blessing to them that love God and unto them who are called according to His purpose. Please do try and send us the Bibles, there are more people turning to Christ, that needed the word of God to grow in the knowledge of Christ.

We are so grateful to the Lord for His inspiration and His pleasant word that bring faith and comfort and for the healing to the sick. May the Lord bless and reward you abundance for your given heart and of your kind gesture unto His lordship. Thanks again for your love and support to the work of His ministry for everybody to be saved. We love and pray for you continuously.

Yours in His vineyard,
EVANG. JOHN ATAKIEL

My Brothers and Sisters that is the power of God. Jesus is there beside you right now saying, Come to me and I will make you fishers of men. Come to me and I will dwell in you and give you my power and authority to be Kings here on earth. Thank you Jesus ... PS: We sent John his Bibles..:-)

Nothing To Offer But My Sinful Heart

From Stella
I should tell you something about Stella, she is from Hong Kong and she did something very bad. She had to go to trial and she was so frightened that she was afraid that she would collapse in the court room. She was hysterical.

We prayed and then I told her what was going to happen. I told her that Jesus was going to be beside her holding her up. That He was bringing two angels with Him and they would be on each side of the Judge. That all she had to do was to admit what she had done and that she was sorry.

I really put Jesus in a box sometimes. Why do I say such things to people? I really think the Holy Spirit puts these things in my heart. But I can back it up.

John 14:13 And whatsoever ye shall ask in my name, that will I do, that the Father may be glorified in the Son.

So I asked Jesus, to help me out and here is the answer I got back from Stella.

Dear Brother Ferd,
Praise to Lord my GOD, I have been saved by my LORD JESUS thank you Lord.My name is Stella and I send my prayer recently to the prayer garden, and I am saved by the LORD MY GOD. My court hearing which took place on the 30th May was discharged. I am so happy that words cannot say how to thank Jesus for coming to the court with me with his two angels.

Brother Ferd thank you so much brother for the prayer and I will always pray for my sisters and brothers in the prayer garden. My case was so serious that I was charged under section 129 and I knew only a miracle can help me. Now I know my JESUS loves all his children. I asked for my LORD's forgiveness for giving my LORD so much sadness in the way I have lived.

PRAISE THE LORD IN THE HIGHEST. THANK YOU 2JESUS FOR MY PRAYER IS BEEN ANSWERED. THANK

YOU I HAVE NOTHING TO OFFER BUT MY SINFUL HEART, LORD MY GOD.
Your daughter
Stella
Jesus was faithful to His Word. He was there for Stella, Ferd

Full of Hate, My Testimony

From Jackie

Dear Ferd, before I got saved life was not much. A lot of stress in my life, Depression. A very unhappy person and felt no one cared about me. I did not even like myself. I have three sons and 3 grandsons and we all love each other much, but it wasn't enough, something was missing. I use to feel God loves everyone, why don't he love me? Why won't he help me?

I would pray but felt it went nowhere. Either God did not hear me or He just didn't care is how I felt. But then I started looking at my life. Everywhere in the Bible it said love. Or means love. I was carrying hate for people, many years of hate. For my sister and brother who I had felt done me wrong and had hurt me.

I would come to your site and I would read a lot. Even copied things and I would sit out side and read what you had written and read the bible. I could not understand why God would bless other people, but when I would pray it just seem to stay the same. I have had health problems, nerve problems and I would pray. But when I would pray some times things even seem to get more worse then better. Then I started reading about the man in the bible who lost everything but would not de-nigh God and in the end he was rewarded. I thought about that, he loved God. He knew love and the most important thing in his life was God.

I got to thinking, I have so much hate in me, how can I love God or even expect him to listen to me. A few days after that my husband and I went shopping and who did I run in to? My brother that I very much disliked. I felt an ache inside of me and a sadness the next thing I knew I walked up to him and hugged him. He pushed back for I knew he still didn't care for me to much but I walked away knowing I had forgiven him and my sister. I walked away knowing I loved them and hope some day that they would love me. I felt a weight lifted and knew I had done the right thing.

The next night I visited your site again and was saved. I left your site knowing it. Now I can truly say I love the lord and he loves me. I know he always loved me but couldn't do a thing tell I could love back and get the hate out. I love the lord Jesus with all my heart and praise him for not giving up on me and my Salvation.

Thank you, Jackie

Jackie, is no longer full of hate. Jesus has filled the void and made her a child of God.

Mark 11:25 And when you stand praying, if you hold anything against anyone, forgive him, so that your Father in heaven may also forgive you your sins ... Ferd@2jesus

A Cry For Help!

From Rev. Julie Squires
   Hi Ferd,
   I just thought I should update you, since my last e-mail, a cry for help. I have found my way in this weary world. I knew, once I started going to church, that God had some wonderful plan in mind for me ... I wasn't sure what. I felt compelled and drawn to him, I felt the love he had for me and the love of my Best Friend and Savior, Jesus Christ. I prayed and prayed that I could do God's will on this Earth. I also prayed for his help and direction. I wanted so much to be a servant of His great Word.
   I am updating you because I have found salvation, I have found happiness. I have found purpose in life. I have been ordained in the Universal Life Church, based in California. I am excited. I have never been so excited about anything in my life. I owe it to you and I owe this to your web site at 2Jesus.
   You have been there for me and with your help and with the love of Jesus, I knew that I was not alone. Ferd, you have been an inspiration to me and your kind words, when I was in trouble and could not find my way, you helped me in so many unimaginable ways... You kept me from doing something that I know I would have regret, suicide.
   I asked you for help. You sent me several bible quotes and you reminded me of the love that Jesus has for me. I know that I will do my best to

be as good of a servant to the Lord as you have.
I will be the best friend I can to all in need, just as
you have been for me.

Ferd, I wrote you to thank you for never giving
up and for your prayers. You have touched my life
and I am so thankful for that.

God Bless, Thank you,

Love, Rev. Julie Squires

I get letters like this and I would like to take the
credit. But it is not me, it is the Words of Jesus that
I give them. If you feel like that life has passed you
by, Never ever give up ... Just look up ... Ferd@2jesus

I Typed in Jesus

From Ruth B. Dreher

Dear Brother Ferd,

I'd like to really thank you for your web site
and your words of wisdom about how to get to
know Jesus, faith, healing, peace. I've suffered
from depression for a long time. Everything I
did took an enormous amount of effort, from
cleaning my room, doing my homework, writing
people, you name it. Getting through school took
an enormous amount of emotional effort, and
I just did enough to get by. Finally, I got married
and had a beautiful little boy. However, I was
overwhelmed and depressed after he was born;
it was hard to take care of him the way I should
have. I couldn't stand to live anymore like this
and I knew I needed help. I really didn't believe
in Jesus until college, and from that time I would
run into Him occasionally when He would help

me out, sometimes in pretty spectacular ways, but I had never made a concerted commitment to Him, probably because I had never become desperate enough.

Well, anyway, I typed in "Jesus" and "Healing" onto an Internet search engine, and up popped "2Jesus" as the first web site. Your site really brought Jesus to life for me, especially your interpretation of the Scriptures about healing, faith, doubt, peace, etc. and the testimonies, Words to Live By, and Inspirational Stories. I started to read the Bible more, pray more, talked to Jesus throughout the day, confess my sins, talked about Jesus to other people, searched for a church to join, and started listening to the Christian radio station. Slowly, bit by bit, my depression lifted over the course of these last few months until it was totally GONE. Thanks to Jesus! I can now do things, anything, with no emotional effort - it's incredible! I just say, Jesus, help me do (whatever), and He helps me! I have never felt so free in my life! Jesus has made me a much better Mom who takes care of and enjoys her child the way she should.

Also, I started praying to God with what I hoped was the kind of faith you described on 2Jesus, especially about healing. My little boy had the same bug bites for weeks that seemed to be getting worse, so I asked God to heal them, and the next day, they were noticeably improved and disappeared within a few days. I had been bickering with my husband and I asked God to help me control my tongue so that I would be kind and loving toward him even if he said and did things that bugged me, and instantly I felt something switch off inside my brain, and from that moment on I've been able to (mostly) control my tongue and say kind things to my husband. It's made a huge improvement to our marriage. Thank you, God! Most recently, my Dad injured his left knee several months ago while working outside, it became swollen, and then the right knee became swollen because of the way my Dad was walking from the injured left knee. His knees remained swollen for about two months and they were becoming painful enough that he was planning on going to the doctor. My Dad, Mom, and I got on the phone and prayed that God would heal my Dad's knees. The next day, the swelling was almost gone, the pain was gone, and within a few days, his knees were as good as new and have been great ever since. Praise the Lord!

Anyway, I finally think that I have started on a journey with Jesus, even though it seems like I'm just beginning. 2Jesus was crucial in getting me started, so thank you so much, Ferd!

Your sister in Christ,
Ruth B. Dreher

It is such a pleasure to see Jesus at work. Ferd

I will FOREVER be thankful to you for your Web Site.

From: Sister Matha Odura
For over 29 years I was nothing but troubled and I wanted nothing to do with GOD. On July

1st 2010, things changed. I accepted JESUS as my Savior. I did not realize how hard it would be to go back out into the world without becoming like the world again.

It took me years to have my eyes opened to the truth. And, this is the truth. If it were not for your web site 2jesus.org, I would have not known the truth and if not for the Pastor of this ministry who showed me your web site and the people in the ministry who sacrificed their time to explain to me all the materials I had printed out from this your web site especially about your testimony on how you got saved, I have no doubts that I would be dead and in hell today.

Now,the LORD has blessed me beyond any words that I can write. He saved me, He gave me a new life and mended my broken relationship with my parents after many years of separation.

I will FOREVER be thankful to you for your web site.

Sister Matha Odura

Sister Matha, was saved by the Word ... Ferd@2jesus

I WANT TO THANK JESUS FOR MY HEALING

From: Nancy (A young lady who had HIV)

I want to thank Jesus for my healing; I know that I am totally healed from the bottom of my heart. My brother in Christ Ferd may God increase you and I wonder if people know about you. From the day you made prayers for me I faced a lot of challenges and I knew it was just to shake me, but

I thank God because I realized that was not true, I told devil that I do not live by what I see or feel but I live by faith and the Grace of God.

I also reminded him that I am what God said I am and it will come to pass because God's word is true if he says I am healed, I am (1Peter 2 - 24).

The truth is there was a battle field, devil tried to bring me down in so many ways, but I refused to go back. As I am writing this I refuse to be inflicted again by any sickness because I have known God and he abides in me so no sickliness / weapon fashioned against me or my children shall prosper. I am thanking God and the devil will not be allowed to steal my healing.

God is working wonders for me and my children; all what was stolen from me is being restored now in the Mighty Name of Jesus Christ of Nazareth. I am a victor and all things works good together for me by the Glory of God. My brother this is only to remind you that I have not forgotten you and I will not forget. Wait I am still coming with more testimonies and I would want God to use me to help other people who were like me because it took me long time to understand God and that he can actually do wonders.

I know I am still learning and I got a long way to read and understand bible and to love God in truth not only seeking him because I have got problems. I think the day I will only manage to love and thank him, my life will be a turn around. I know he loves me because I know where I am coming from and he was so patient with me. I LOVE JESUS and I THANK YOU MY BROTHER FERD because with your teaching everything opens.

MAY GOD BLESS YOU AND INCREASE YOU, BROTHER FERD

Nancy, will soon be a Mighty Soldier of the Cross. Ferd

Thank You, Brother Ferd

From: Nikki
Brother Ferd!
Thank you very much to hear me out for all those days! I cannot thank you enough for your encouragement and support in the name of Jesus. Brother Ferd today was the first time I prayed with my mother in the name of Jesus!!!

Hallelujah!!! There is power in the name of Jesus and His blood. Oh I love Him so much!!! Brother Ferd we have been going through some difficult times, and today I just had this very strong in my heart the Holy Spirit leading me to pray for my mother and with her and we did and I feel so happy I know that my prayer is already answered! There have been other prayers that I have prayed like for the health of my grandmother who is living very far from us. And it is absolutely miraculous how she was saved... She had gotten really sick but because of my Father in Heaven she lives healthy today... I am so happy I just want my Father God to get the glory because its all His. We are all His! I never knew there was so much power available to followers of Jesus. If only we Believe!! I am ecstatic right now!! hehe.

Thank you very much,
I just really wanted to share this with you.
You are in my prayers.
Nikki
Nikki, loves Jesus ... Because He first loved her ... Ferd@2jesus

A Note from Will

From Will Bane
Hi Ferd
I just wanted to tell you how I feel about My Lord Jesus. I feel so blessed and am blessed because He has been answering my prayers and I know He lives and is my best friend. I had a spur in my heal and it was getting very painful so I asked Jesus to heal me and thank the Lord I have no pain now.

I have been learning how to ask Jesus for what I want, I was afraid to ask Him for any big thing because I didn't think He would give me such a large request. Not any more, they were big for me but not for my Jesus.

I know you are about the Lords business because of all the healing He has done for you but also because of the mansion He is building for you in glory.

It really is such a great feeling not to have to worry about things or how tomorrow is going to turn out; it is such a relief to know no matter what it brings it will be alright.

Thank you Ferd, for being the man God wanted you to be in His service.
Will Bane

The feeling is mutual. I think Will, is the kind of man God wanted him to be also. .Ferd@2jesus

Hallelujah!!!

From Barbara
Dear Saints, Hallelujah!!! God has healed me. What an awesome God we serve. He has lifted me from the depths of death and has restored my soul. Glory to God. Thank you saints for your prayers ... God has heard them and has answered them. I am so grateful to all who have prayed for me. He has healed my body and I am confident that my other needs have already been provided for by Him. May God bless you and those you love with every good thing according to the riches of His glory in Christ Jesus. Amen.
Your sister in Christ Jesus, Barbara
PS: It was Cancer, that Barbara got healed from. Thank you Jesus ... Ferd@2jesus

Good Morning Ferd

From Sandy
Good morning Ferd,
Just a short note to thank you and Jesus for the healing you did for my landscaper, Rick. He is here today and he told me he is healed! No more cancer. We thanked Jesus and I just wanted you to know that your healing session with him was what did it. He is fine, working hard and no residual effects at all. God bless you. His Assistant, Ann has

visited your site many times and thanks you too. Love, Sandy

Give Jesus the praise and glory ... Ferd@2jesus

Jesus Is My Lover

From Robert
   I would like to thank the Lord Jesus for his saving me from severe mental illness, severe anxiety, paranoia and mistrust of the whole world. I hated the world and suffered extreme depression, after suffering years of psychosomatic illness and bizarre symptoms and suffering shame, after years of suffering guilt from being bullied and suffering in silence with homosexuality. I am now free from all psychosomatic illness, anxiety, fear and no longer feel lonely and the need to have a partner because I have Jesus as my lover. Praise God and never give up, I thought I would never come through my illness and negative thinking but now I think positively because of God. I now live at peace with God and all men once more. Thank you Jesus!
   Jesus is Love and He shares it so Beautifully, Ferd

AN 8 LB. 13 OZ. MIRACLE

From: Jett and Valerie
   This letter is from a young couple with a big decision. You will notice here that they were praying for themselves, wanting God to show them which path to take.

Brother Ferd

Please pray for my husband and me. We had an ultrasound for our 2nd baby yesterday and there is great possibility of fetal abnormalities.

Thank you,

Jett and Valerie

This was the Doctors way of saying now is the time to abort if you wish ... Here is 2jesus answer back.

Dear Jett and Valerie,

Phil 4:6-7

6 Be careful for nothing; but in every thing by prayer and supplication with thanksgiving let your requests be made known unto God.

7 And the peace of God, which passes all understanding, shall keep your hearts and minds through Christ Jesus.

Dear Parents, read the above verse carefully. We give our worry to God ... With thanksgiving. Why thanksgiving? Because He is now in control and we know that He knows how to fix our problem. Then what will happen? We can rest and be at peace and keep the worry and fear from our minds.

Now let us do our part. Jett, you and your wife put your hands on her stomach. In my spirit I will be there with you and my hand will be on yours. Say this prayer aloud as this child is being wonderfully healed.

Dear Father, we have a problem that only you can handle for us. Jesus said, John 16:23, Verily,

verily, I say unto you, Whatsoever ye shall ask the Father in my name, he will give it to you. Thank you Jesus. Father we believe Jesus words. They are in our hearts and on our mind. Father we are asking now in the name of Jesus to have the Holy Spirit touch this child. Make this child perfect. Father after this child is born, let the world see the glory radiating out of this baby so that the world will know, this is a child of God and it will always be a reminder of the power and love of Jesus Christ for the rest of it's life. Father, we praise you and thank you in Jesus precious name. Your loving children, Jett, Valerie and Ferd ... Amen.

I do not care what the Drs say from this day on, your child will be perfect, so continue to praise God for your perfect baby, because by Jesus stripes your child is healed. Be sure and give me a report after the baby is born. I always love to see how Jesus can bring His glory to every situation.

Your brother in Christ, Ferd@2jesus

---

5 Months later this answer came.

Dear Ferd,

I wanted to let you know that on Monday, March 9th our daughter was born. She weighed 8lbs and 13oz and is 18 inches long. She is the perfect gift from God. She is a very healthy and normal baby girl. Thank you so much for praying with us during my pregnancy and helping us realize that the only person we ever needed in our lives for guidance and comfort was the Lord.

I've enclosed a picture of our daughter Lorelai DeAnn Pilcher.
With love,
Valerie and Jett

Dear Valerie,
Praise God!
All things are possible if we only believe.
Thank you Jesus.
God bless you, Valerie, Jett and Lorelai DeAnn.
Your brother in Christ, Ferd

Here is Lorelai DeAnn

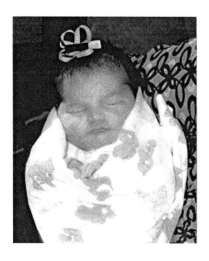

The Value of Divine Healing

The value of divine healing is not just that people
are healed.....
The real value is much greater...
It becomes a demonstration of the Power of God,
that dwells in every believer's life...
So that we, feeling His awesome power, in our
bodies,
will have full knowledge, of the Holy Spirit.
And make us, mighty men in the hands of Jesus!
Making us, true sons and daughters of God.

HALLELUJAH!

We have hundreds of stories of Jesus Power on
2jesus.org. Visit us and we will Praise God together.
He loves you so much; He has so many gifts for
you. Look at this prayer, just for you...

Eph 3:16-21
16 I pray that out of his glorious riches he may
strengthen you with power through his Spirit in your
inner being,

17 so that Christ may dwell in your hearts through
faith. And I pray that you, being rooted and
established in love,

18 may have power, together with all the saints,
to grasp how wide and long and high and deep is
the love of Christ,

19 and to know this love that surpasses knowledge-- that you may be filled to the measure of all the fullness of God.

20 Now to him who is able to do immeasurably more than all we ask or imagine, according to his power that is at work within us,

21 to him be glory in the church and in Christ Jesus throughout all generations, for ever and ever! Amen.

I just could not give you
a better present than that!
In Christ's Love, Your Brother, Ferd

CPSIA information can be obtained at www.ICGtesting.com
Printed in the USA
BVOW081025310712

296669BV00011B/27/P